DOUGAL DIXON'S

AMAZING DINOSAURS

The Fiercest, the Tallest, the Toughest, the Smallest

Boyds Mills Press

Published by Caroline House
Boyds Mills Press, Inc.
A Highlights Company
815 Church Street
Honesdale, Pennsylvania 18431

Printed in Hong Kong

U.S. Cataloging-in-Publication Data
(Library of Congress Standards)

Dixon, Dougal.
Amazing Dinosaurs : the fiercest, the tallest, the toughest, the smallest / by Dougal Dixon.
[128] p. : col. Ill. ; cm.
Includes index and glossary.
Summary: Descriptions of the strangest and the most famous dinosaurs, including new discoveries.
ISBN 1-56397-773-7
[1. Dinosaurs. 2. Paleontology.] I. Title
567.9 / 1 dc21 2000 AC CIP
99-65298

First edition, 2000

Book designed and produced by
Bender Richardson White
Uxbridge, England

Art Director, Designer: Ben White
Managing Editor: Lionel Bender
Text Editors: Sue Nicholson, Andy Boyles
Production: Kim Richardson
Electronic Page Makeup: MW Graphics
Illustrations by Steve Kirk, Chris Forsey, James Field, Jim Robins, John James.

The text of this book is set in Imago and Joanna.

10 9 8 7 6 5 4 3 2

About This Book

The dinosaurs roamed the Earth for millions of years. Some were tiny. Others were the biggest land animals ever to have lived. Scientists recognize six different types of dinosaur, and that is how we have divided up this book. The first section deals with the meat-eaters—the dinosaurs that scientists call **theropods**. The second section looks at the long-necked plant-eaters, or **sauropods**. In the third part, we look at the three different types of dinosaur that carried armor—the plate-backed **stegosaurs**, the armored **ankylosaurs**, and the horned **ceratopsians**. The final part of the book is about the two-footed plant-eaters, or **ornithopods**. Altogether, these dinosaurs represent the most fascinating group of animals that ever lived.

Author Dougal Dixon is an internationally recognized authority on dinosaurs. He is one of the most popular science writers in Great Britain and the author of more than twenty books about dinosaurs, a number of them for young readers. His titles include *The Age of Dinosaurs*, *The Macmillan Illustrated Encyclopedia of Dinosaurs and Prehistoric Animals*, and the award-winning *Dougal Dixon's Dinosaurs*, published by Boyds Mills Press.

Scientific Advisor Dr. Peter Dodson is a professor of anatomy and geology at the University of Pennsylvania School of Veterinary Medicine and a research associate of the Academy of Natural Sciences of Philadelphia. He has studied dinosaurs in Canada, the United States, India, Madagascar, and China.

Contents

The Meat-Eaters

Long-Necked Plant-Eaters

Armored Dinosaurs

Two-Footed Plant-Eaters

Reference Section

Dinosaur Family Tree

The word dinosaur comes from Latin words and means "terrible lizard." Some dinosaurs were fierce and did look like present-day lizards. But others looked like different kinds of reptiles, such as crocodiles, or they resembled mammals or birds. In fact, birds are the closest living relatives of the dinosaurs.

The idea we all have of dinosaurs is often that of the "terrible lizard," like this *Allosaurus*.

How were dinosaurs related to one another? The meat-eating dinosaurs were all closely related, just as present-day lions, tigers, and house cats are relatives. In turn, the meat-eating dinosaurs were related to the long-necked plant-eaters and more distantly related to the two-footed plant-eaters and the armored dinosaurs. Page five shows the dinosaur family tree.

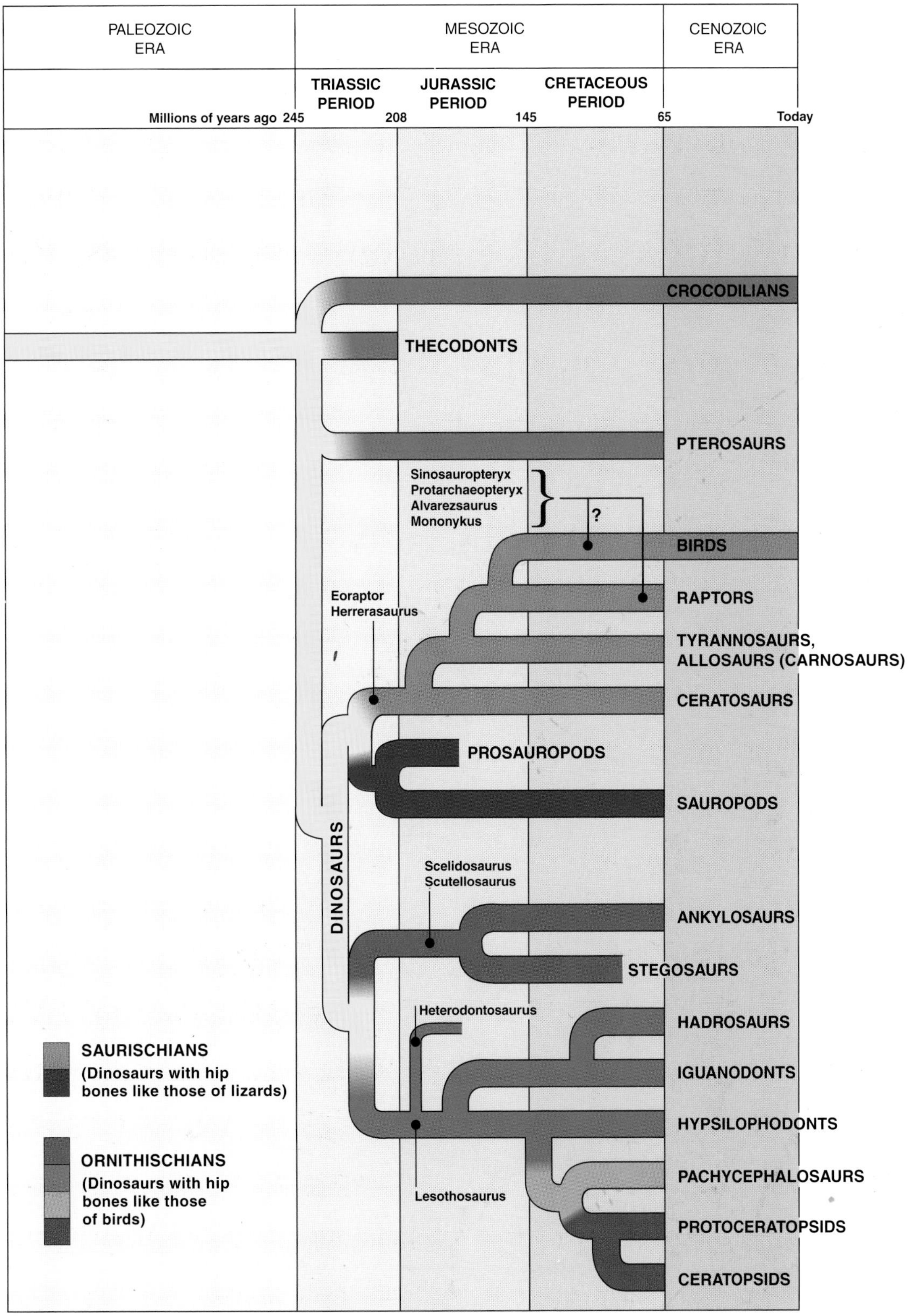
PALEOZOIC ERA
MESOZOIC ERA
CENOZOIC ERA
TRIASSIC PERIOD
JURASSIC PERIOD
CRETACEOUS PERIOD
Millions of years ago 245
208
145
65
Today
CROCODILIANS
THECODONTS
PTEROSAURS
Sinosauropteryx
Protarchaeopteryx
Alvarezsaurus
Mononykus
?
BIRDS
RAPTORS
Eoraptor
Herrerasaurus
TYRANNOSAURS, ALLOSAURS (CARNOSAURS)
CERATOSAURS
PROSAUROPODS
SAUROPODS
DINOSAURS
Scelidosaurus
Scutellosaurus
ANKYLOSAURS
STEGOSAURS
Heterodontosaurus
HADROSAURS
IGUANODONTS
HYPSILOPHODONTS
Lesothosaurus
PACHYCEPHALOSAURS
PROTOCERATOPSIDS
CERATOPSIDS
SAURISCHIANS
(Dinosaurs with hip bones like those of lizards)
ORNITHISCHIANS
(Dinosaurs with hip bones like those of birds)

The Meat-Eaters

The earliest dinosaurs appeared in South America 228 million years ago. There, they shared the landscape with all kinds of other **reptiles**. Two of these early dinosaurs were meat-eaters. They would have eaten the plant-eating reptiles.

A plant-eating reptile, the size of a modern-day pig, has just been killed by a new kind of animal—the dinosaur *Herrerasaurus*. A larger meat-eating reptile and a small dinosaur, *Eoraptor*, come to take a share of the kill.

KEY

1 *Herrerasaurus*
2 *Eoraptor*

1
2

Inside Story

Allosaurus (AL-o-SAW-rus) was the biggest and most common of all the meat-eating dinosaurs that lived at the end of the **Jurassic** Period, around 165 to 145 million years ago. It was built like other meat-eaters, with strong legs and jaws.

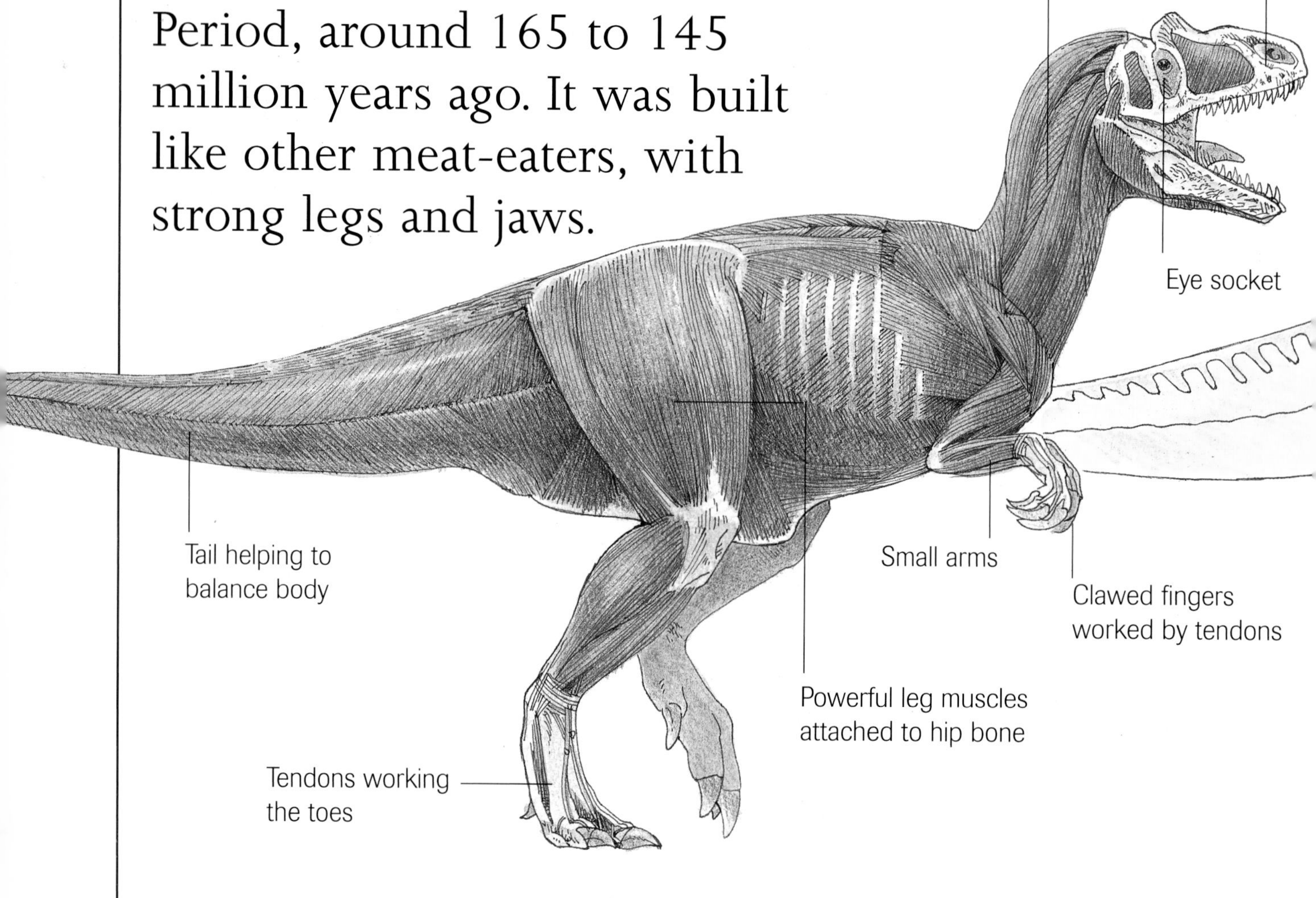

Powerful Muscles
Allosaurus ran on its powerful hind legs. Its biggest leg muscles were high up on each thigh. This was ideal for running fast and hunting. *Allosaurus* also had strong neck and jaw muscles.

Strong Claws and Jaws
Allosaurus could curl its fingers like a pincer. It had strong claws to grab and kill its **prey**. Its long jaws contained rows of sharp teeth for tearing through meat.

EXTERNAL EVIDENCE

The soft, outside parts of a dinosaur do not often become fossils. But we think that *Allosaurus* had large claws on its fingers and scales on its body. Its color pattern might have been like a large lizard's or even a tiger's.

Lung Power

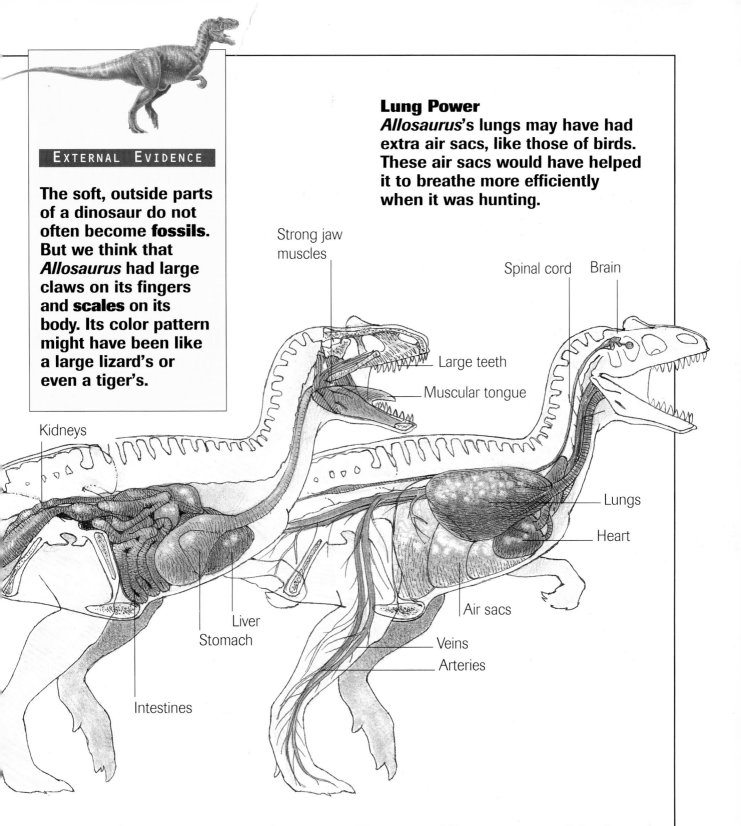

***Allosaurus*'s lungs may have had extra air sacs, like those of birds. These air sacs would have helped it to breathe more efficiently when it was hunting.**

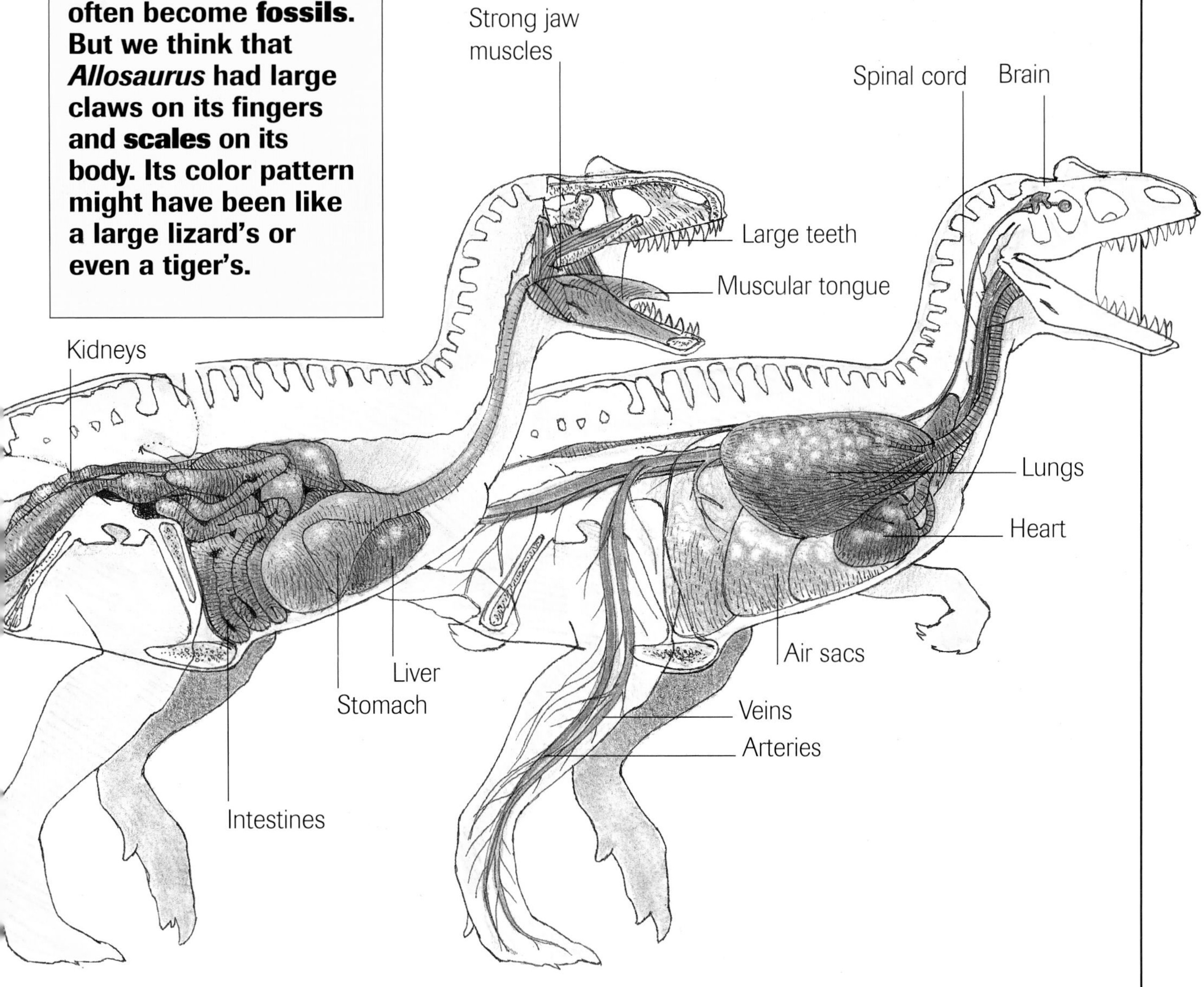

Digestive Organs

***Allosaurus* had short intestines because meat is easier to digest than plant food. (Because plants are harder to digest, plant-eaters need bigger stomachs and longer intestines.) This gave *Allosaurus* a small body compared with plant-eaters around at the same time. For this reason, even today meat-eaters, such as tigers and wolves, are usually smaller than plant-eaters, such as wildebeests.**

Starting Small

Facts and Figures

Eoraptor
(EE-o-RAP-tur)
Meaning of Name: "Dawn thief"—hunted for food at the start of the Age of Dinosaurs
Classification: Uncertain, but probably a group from which the theropods evolved
Size, Weight: 3 feet (1 meter) long, 11–16 pounds (5–7 kilograms)
Time: Late Triassic, 228 million years ago
Place: Northwestern Argentina
Food: Meat, insects

Herrerasaurus
(huh-RARE-uh-SAW-rus)
Meaning of Name: "Herrera's lizard"—named after its discoverer, Victorino Herrera
Classification: Herrerasaur—a family that evolved before the rest of the meat-eaters
Size, Weight: 10–20 feet (3–6 meters) long, 800–1,000 pounds (360–460 kilograms)
Time: Late Triassic, 228 million years ago
Place: Northwestern Argentina
Food: Meat

Eoraptor
Eoraptor **preyed on other reptiles and may have eaten smaller animals, such as insects. Like modern reptiles, it probably had scaly skin and laid eggs.**

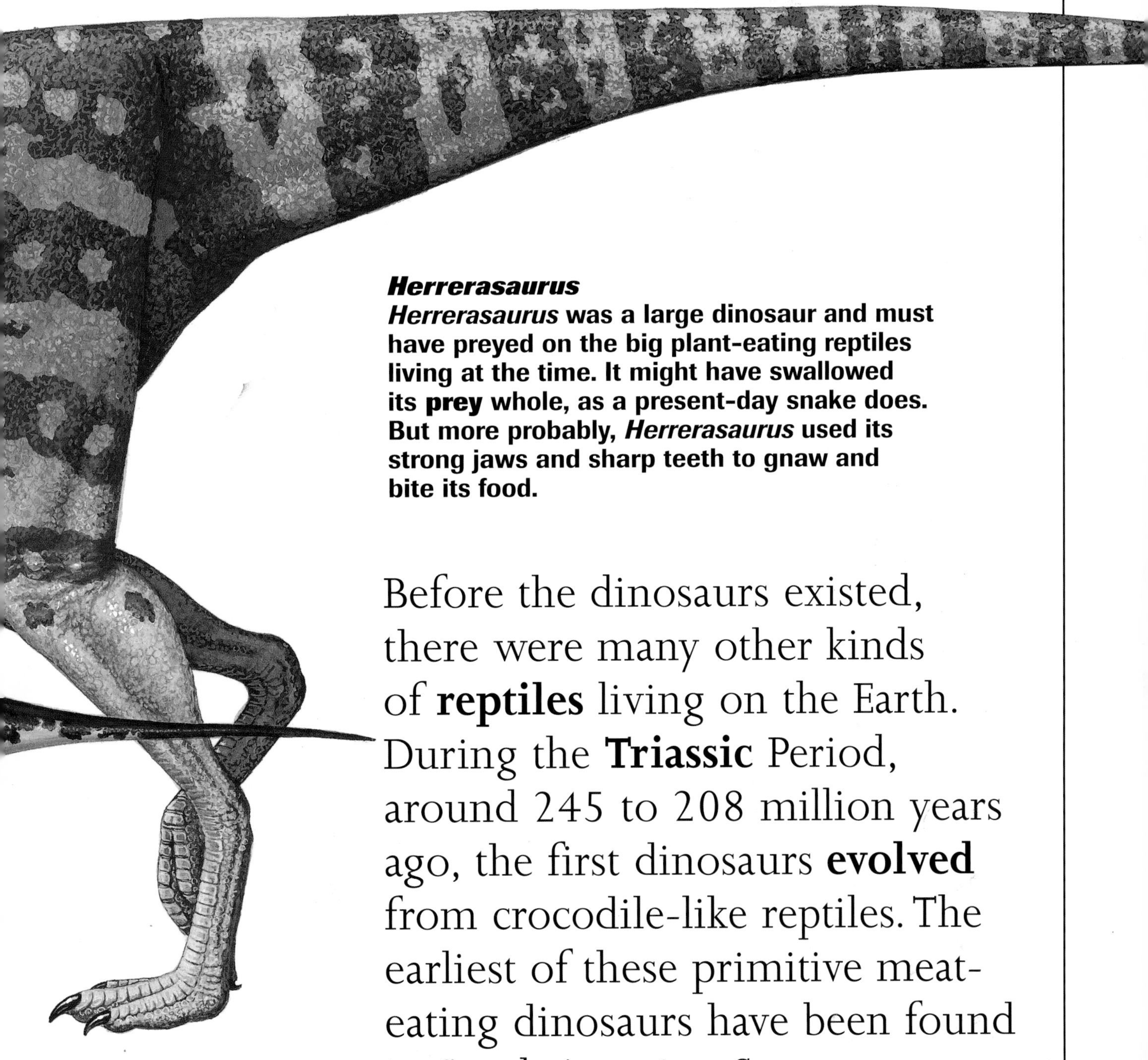

Herrerasaurus
Herrerasaurus **was a large dinosaur and must have preyed on the big plant-eating reptiles living at the time. It might have swallowed its prey whole, as a present-day snake does. But more probably, *Herrerasaurus* used its strong jaws and sharp teeth to gnaw and bite its food.**

Before the dinosaurs existed, there were many other kinds of **reptiles** living on the Earth. During the **Triassic** Period, around 245 to 208 million years ago, the first dinosaurs **evolved** from crocodile-like reptiles. The earliest of these primitive meat-eating dinosaurs have been found in South America. Some were small—about the size of large lizards found today. Others were as big and fierce as tigers.

Pack Hunters

Some meat-eating dinosaurs hunted alone. Others hunted in packs, as wolves do today. A pack of small animals can easily hunt a much larger, slower animal. Together, the animals in a pack can attack a big plant-eater from all sides, killing it with many slashes and bites.

Coelophysis
Hundreds of *Coelophysis* skeletons were found in a quarry in New Mexico. All the animals in the pack were gathered around a water hole that had dried up in a drought.

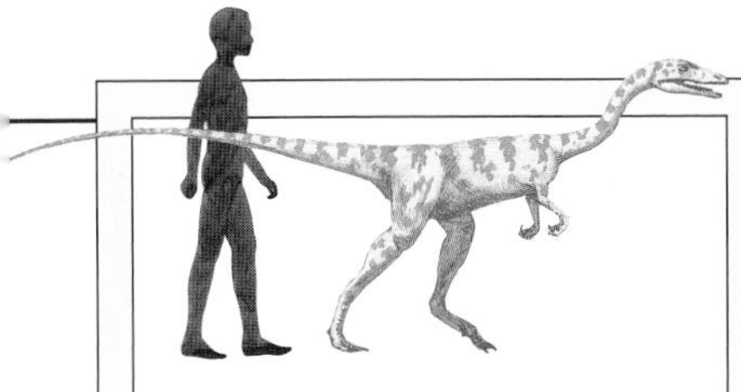

FACTS AND FIGURES

Coelophysis
(SEE-lo-FY-sis)
Meaning of Name: "Hollow form"—because of its hollow bones
Classification: Ceratosaur—a primitive group of meat-eating dinosaurs, some with horns on their noses
Size, Weight: Up to 9 feet (3 meters) long, 40 pounds (18 kilograms)
Time: Late Triassic, 225 million years ago
Place: Southwest United States
Food: Meat, especially smaller reptiles

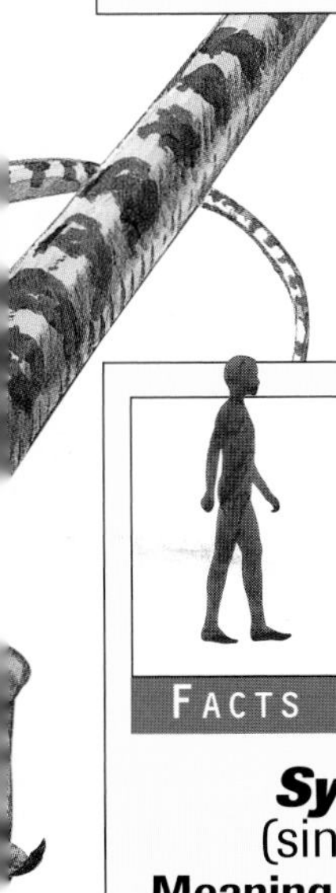

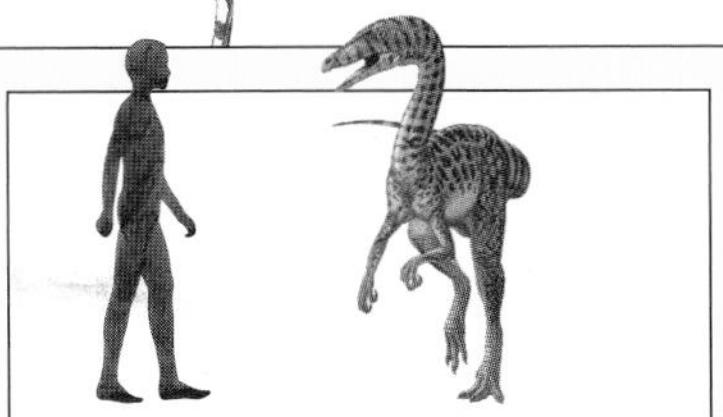

FACTS AND FIGURES

Syntarsus
(sin-TAR-sus)
Meaning of Name: "Ankle stuck together"—from its foot bones, which were joined
Classification: Ceratosaur
Size, Weight: 10 feet (3 meters) long, 50 pounds (23 kilograms)
Time: Early Jurassic, 200 million years ago
Place: Zimbabwe, East Africa, and Arizona
Food: Meat, probably smaller reptiles

Syntarsus

Syntarsus **lived in Africa while the very similar** ***Coelophysis*** **lived in North America. This shows that the two continents of Africa and North America were joined during the Early Jurassic Period and that the same kinds of dinosaurs lived all over the world.**

Crested Killers

Many meat-eating dinosaurs had spectacular **crests** on their heads. These probably helped them to recognize one another, especially at mating time. Some crests had heavy bones in the middle. These crests may have been used when the animals were fighting one another for mates.

Cryolophosaurus
(CRY-o-LO-fo-SAW-rus)
Meaning of Name: "Frozen crested lizard"—found in the icy Antarctic
Classification: Ceratosaur
Size, Weight: 25 feet (8 meters) long, 1,500 pounds (680 kilograms)
Time: Early Jurassic, 200 million years ago

FACTS AND FIGURES

Place: Antarctica
Food: Meat, perhaps other dinosaurs

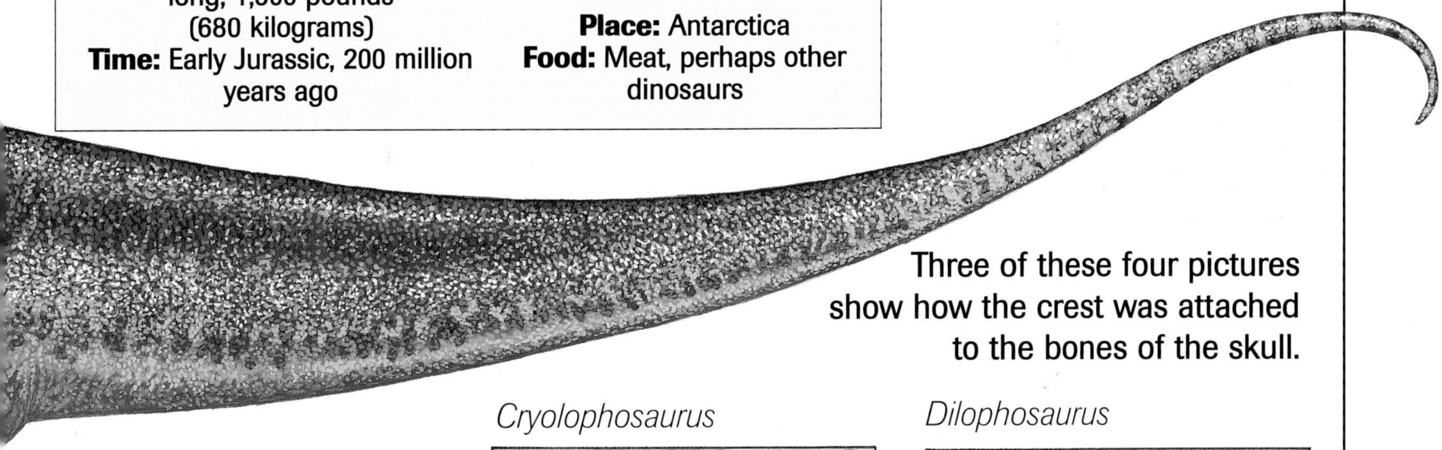

Three of these four pictures show how the crest was attached to the bones of the skull.

Cryolophosaurus

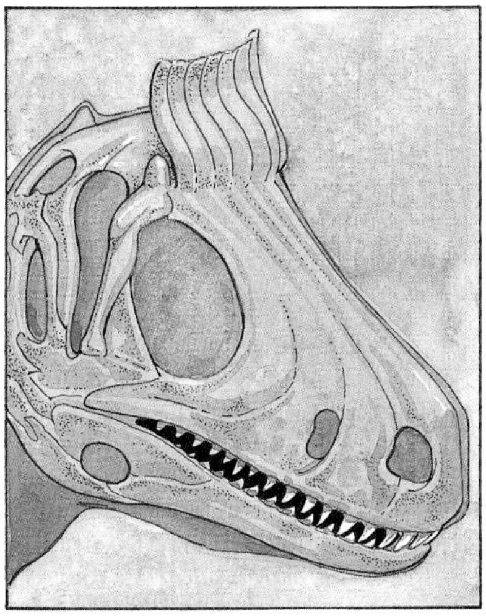

Dilophosaurus

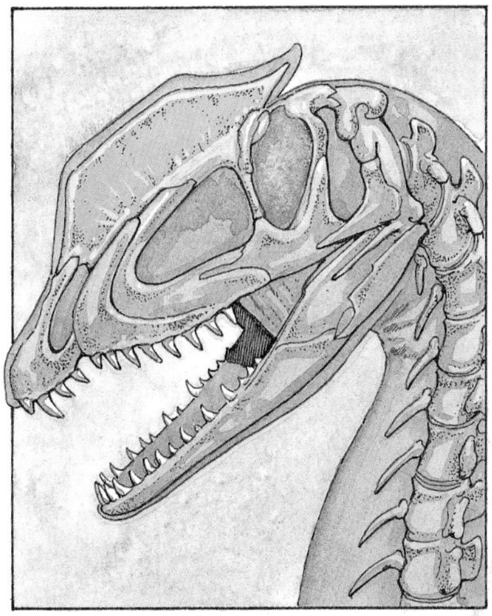

Monolophosaurus

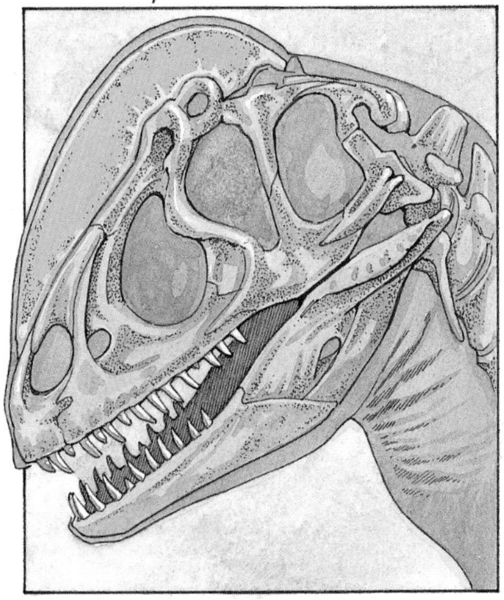

Carnotaurus

Cryolophosaurus
Cryolophosaurus was one of the first dinosaurs to be discovered in Antarctica. Since it was a meat-eater, there must have been other dinosaurs living in Antarctica, too.

Dilophosaurus
Dilophosaurus was a lightly built animal with two crests on its head.

Monolophosaurus
Monolophosaurus had a single, hollow crest that may have helped to cool the dinosaur's head.

Carnotaurus
Carnotaurus may have used its bull-like horns as weapons, to fight rivals for territory or a mate.

Giant-Killer

Allosaurus was the biggest and fiercest meat-eating dinosaur of the Late **Jurassic** Period. In the rocks of the time, scientists have found skeletons of plant-eaters that have been torn apart with great ferocity. There are deep grooves in the bones scored by the teeth of large **carnivores** like *Allosaurus*. Broken *Allosaurus* teeth are scattered around.

FACTS AND FIGURES

Allosaurus
(AL-oh-SAW-rus)
Meaning of Name: "Different reptile"–different from other reptiles that had been found
Classification: Allosaur
Size, Weight: 25 feet (8 meters) long, 3,300 pounds (1,500 kilograms)
Time: Late Jurassic, 156 to 145 million years ago
Place: Western North America
Food: Other dinosaurs

The Prey

Allosaurus hunted the plant-eating dinosaurs that lived at the end of the Jurassic Period. These included the two-footed plant-eaters, such as _Camptosaurus_, shown below (as dead prey) and at right.

Allosaurus

Allosaurus hooked its three-clawed hands into the skin of its prey, then bit it with its huge mouth to finish the kill. Its teeth had saw-like rear edges to tear through skin and bone.

Fish-Eaters

Not all meat-eating dinosaurs hunted and killed big animals. An Early **Cretaceous** group called the spinosaurs seemed to be well adapted for hunting fish, with long jaws and large claws. They probably waded into rivers and hooked the fish with their claws, just as grizzly bears do today.

Spinosaurs
The whole group of spinosaurs take their name from *Spinosaurus*.

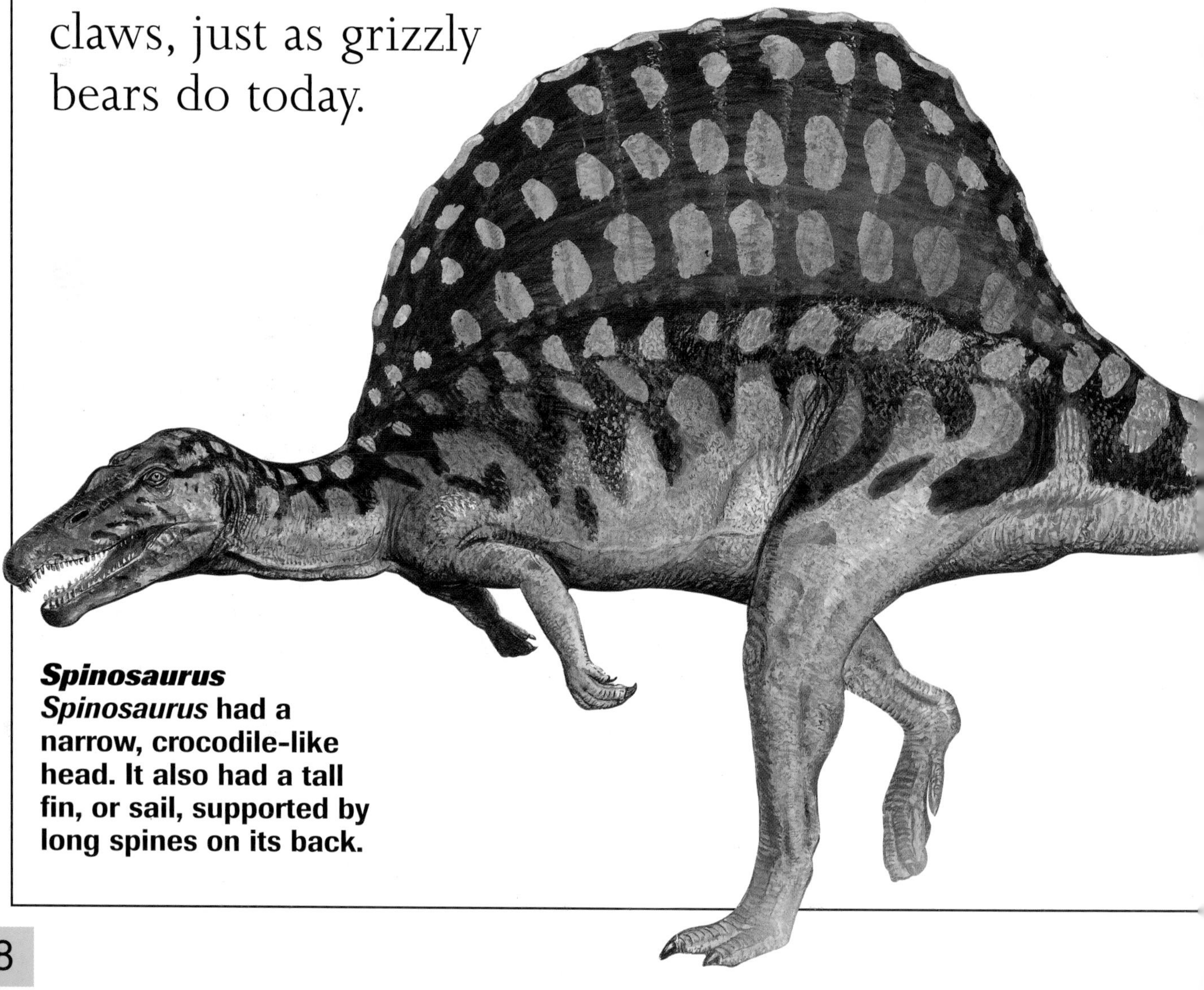

Spinosaurus
***Spinosaurus* had a narrow, crocodile-like head. It also had a tall fin, or sail, supported by long spines on its back.**

Baryonyx

Only one skeleton of *Baryonyx* has ever been discovered. Fish scales and bones were found in its stomach—remains of its last meal.

aryonyx had long, crocodile-like aws with thirty-two teeth on ach side.

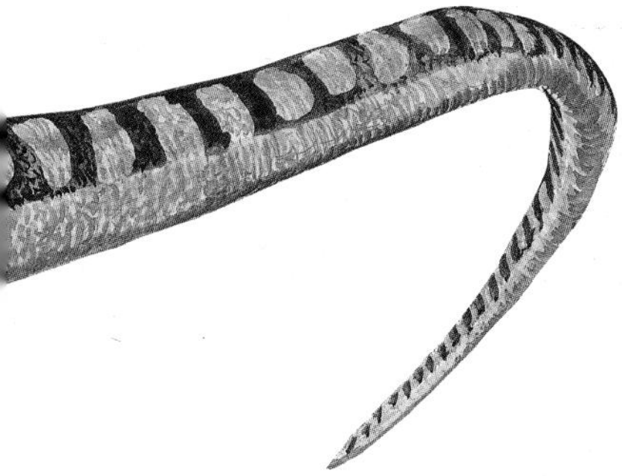

FACTS AND FIGURES

Spinosaurus

(SPY-nuh-SAW-rus)

Meaning of Name: "Spined lizard"—from the spines down its back

Classification: Carnosaur

Size, Weight: 40 feet (12 meters) long, 4 tons (3,600 kilograms)

Time: Beginning of the Late Cretaceous, 90 million years ago

Place: Egypt

Food: Fish

FACTS AND FIGURES

Baryonyx

(BEAR-ee-ON-icks)

Meaning of Name: "Heavy claw"—had a large claw on its thumb

Classification: Carnosaur

Size, Weight: 30 feet (9 meters) long, 3,300 pounds (1,500 kilograms)

Time: Early Cretaceous, 125 million years ago

Place: Southern England

Food: Fish

Fast Killers

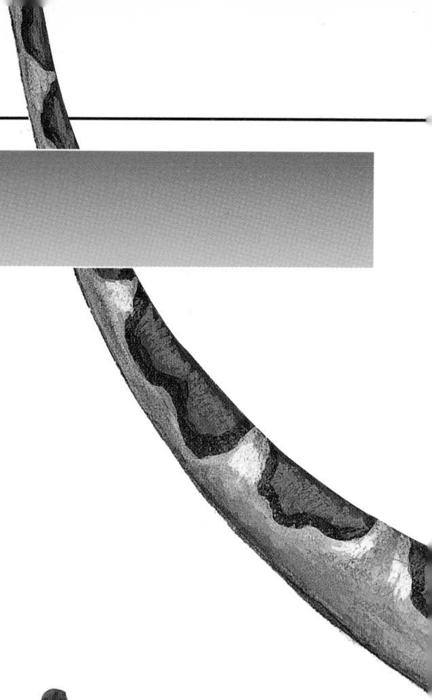

Probably the most fearsome of the hunting dinosaurs were the dromaeosaurs, or "raptors." These were all fast-running animals with long grasping fingers and big claws on their hind feet. They did not kill other animals quickly. Instead, they slashed deep wounds into the sides of their **prey** and then let it bleed to death.

FACTS AND FIGURES

Velociraptor
(veh-LAW-sih-RAP-tur)
Meaning of Name: "Fast thief"—a quick hunter
Classification: Raptor
Size, Weight: 6 feet (2 meters) long, 30 pounds (14 kilograms)
Time: Late Cretaceous, 80 million years ago
Place: Mongolia and China
Food: Small animals, including dinosaurs

Velociraptor
If you tickle a cat's chest, it holds on to your hand with its front paws and kicks with its hind legs. In 1971, scientists found the skeleton of a *Velociraptor* holding on to the skeleton of a *Protoceratops* in the same way. They had killed each other in a fight.

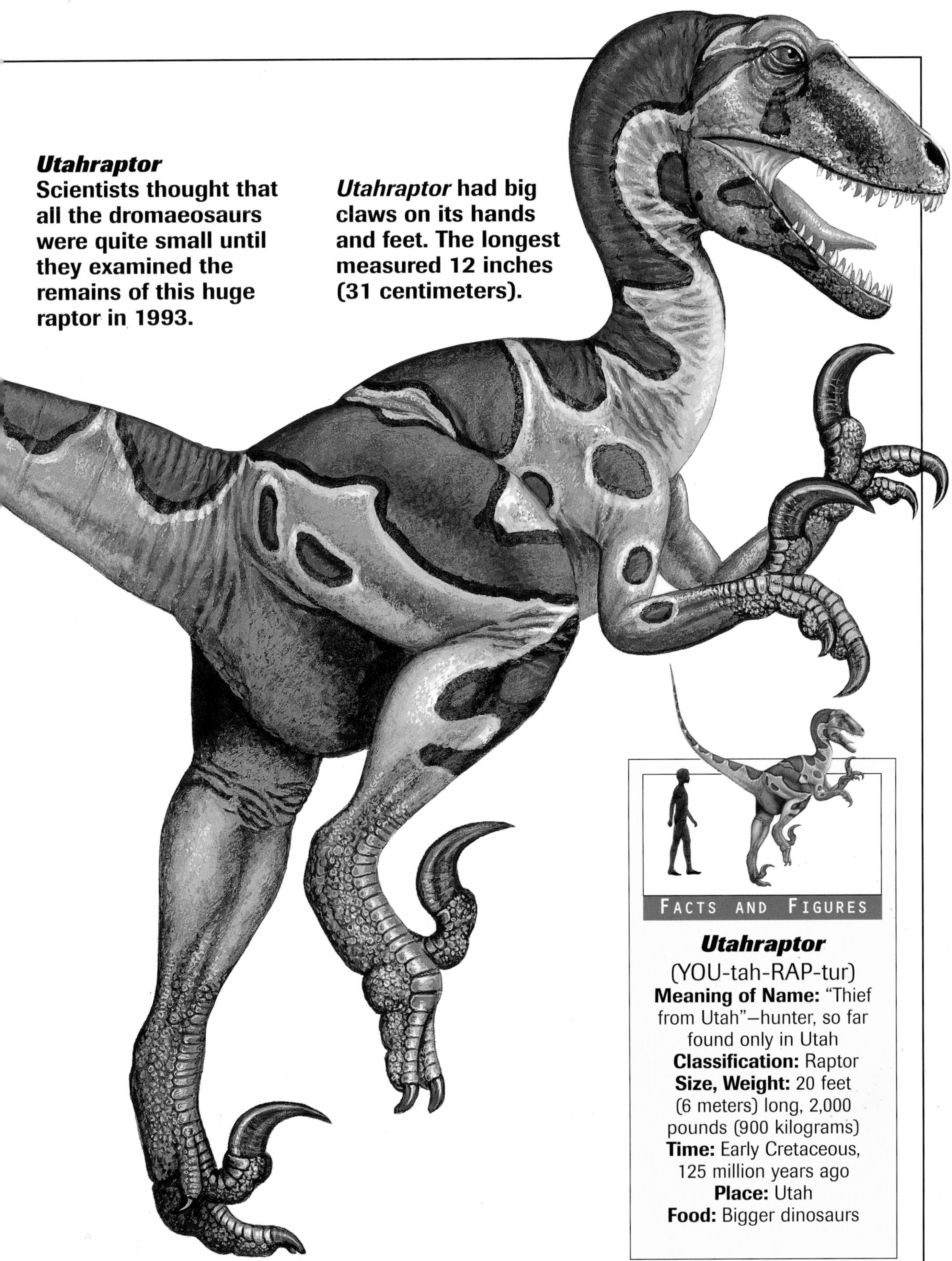

Utahraptor
Scientists thought that all the dromaeosaurs were quite small until they examined the remains of this huge raptor in 1993.

***Utahraptor* had big claws on its hands and feet. The longest measured 12 inches (31 centimeters).**

FACTS AND FIGURES

Utahraptor
(YOU-tah-RAP-tur)
Meaning of Name: "Thief from Utah"—hunter, so far found only in Utah
Classification: Raptor
Size, Weight: 20 feet (6 meters) long, 2,000 pounds (900 kilograms)
Time: Early Cretaceous, 125 million years ago
Place: Utah
Food: Bigger dinosaurs

Dinosaurs to Birds

Archaeopteryx, discovered about 140 years ago, had a skeleton like that of a dinosaur and feathers and wings like those of a bird. It has always been thought of as the best proof that birds **evolved** from dinosaurs. Then, in the late 1990s, scientists discovered more proof—fossil animals that were part bird and part dinosaur.

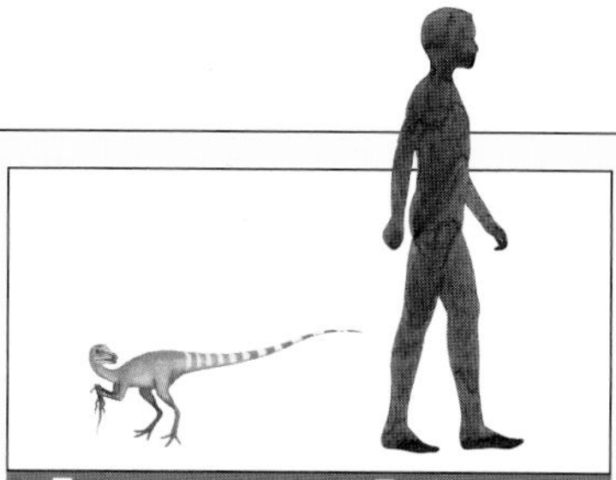

FACTS AND FIGURES

Sinosauropteryx
(SYE-noh-sawr-OP-tair-icks)
Meaning of Name: "Winged lizard from China"
Classification: Uncertain, but somewhere between theropods and birds
Size, Weight: 3 feet (1 meter) long, 9 pounds (5 kilograms)
Time: Early Cretaceous, 124 million years ago
Place: Liaoning Province, China
Food: Insects, small reptiles

Sinosauropteryx
***Sinosauropteryx* was a small meat-eating dinosaur. Its skin was covered with fine hair-like fibers.**

It seems unlikely that any of these animals could fly. Their coverings may have helped to keep them warm, or they may have been used to attract a mate, like the bright tail feathers of a male peacock.

Protarchaeopteryx
***Protarchaeopteryx* was covered in small downy feathers. It also had longer feathers on its arms and a fan of long feathers on its tail.**

FACTS AND FIGURES

Protarchaeopteryx
(PROH-tar-kee-OP-tair-icks)
Meaning of Name: "First ancient wing"—an early bird
Classification: Uncertain
Size, Weight: 3 feet (1 meter) long, 9 pounds (4 kilograms)
Time: Early Cretaceous, 124 million years ago
Place: Liaoning Province, China
Food: Insects, small reptiles

Caudipteryx
***Caudipteryx* had long feathers on its arms and tail. It had few teeth and a bird-like beak.**

FACTS AND FIGURES

Caudipteryx
(caw-DIP-tair-icks)
Meaning of Name: "Tail-wing"
Classification: Uncertain
Size: Just over 3 feet (1meter) long, around 12 pounds (5 kilograms)
Time: Early Cretaceous, 124 million years ago
Place: Liaoning Province, China
Food: Insects, small reptiles

Single Claws

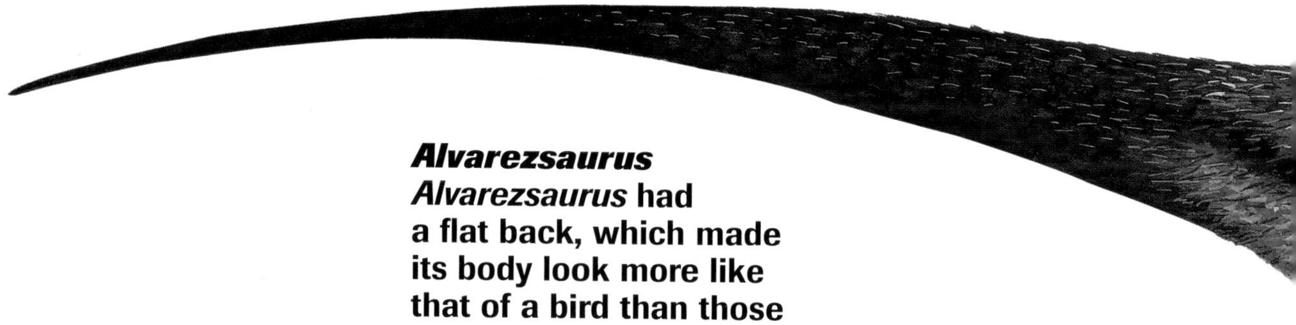

Alvarezsaurus
***Alvarezsaurus* had a flat back, which made its body look more like that of a bird than those of other dinosaurs.**

Even today, scientists do not know whether the alvarezsaurs were dinosaurs or birds. They were built like other lightweight, meat-eating dinosaurs, but their arms were short and powerful, and they had only one usable claw. Scientists are not sure what these strange arms were used for. Perhaps they were for digging. Or they could be the **vestiges** of wings. Perhaps the alvarezsaurs were birds that had lost their powers of flight. We do not know whether they had feathers.

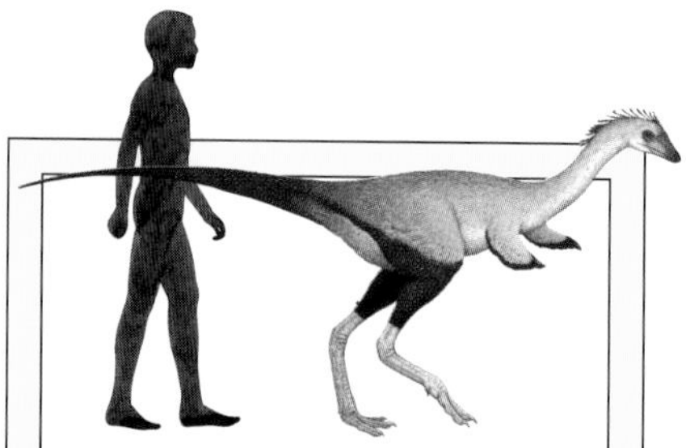

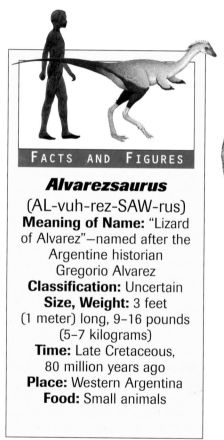

FACTS AND FIGURES

Alvarezsaurus
(AL-vuh-rez-SAW-rus)
Meaning of Name: "Lizard of Alvarez"—named after the Argentine historian Gregorio Alvarez
Classification: Uncertain
Size, Weight: 3 feet (1 meter) long, 9–16 pounds (5–7 kilograms)
Time: Late Cretaceous, 80 million years ago
Place: Western Argentina
Food: Small animals

FACTS AND FIGURES

Mononykus
(MAW-no-NY-kus)
Meaning of Name: "Single claw"—because of its one usable claw
Classification: Uncertain
Size, Weight: 30 inches (76 centimeters) long, 9 pounds (4 kilograms)
Time: Late Cretaceous, 85 to 75 million years ago
Place: Mongolia
Food: Small animals and insects

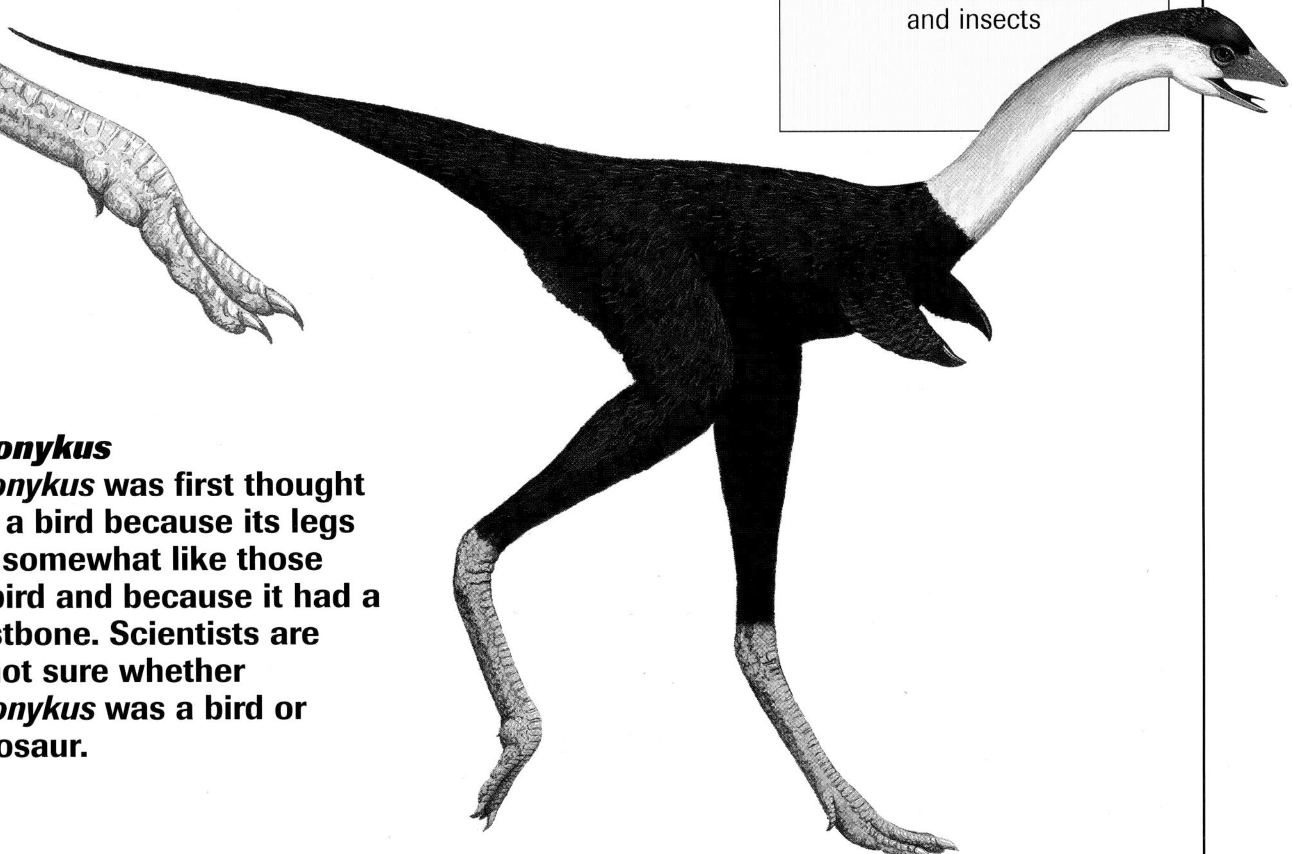

Mononykus
Mononykus **was first thought to be a bird because its legs were somewhat like those of a bird and because it had a breastbone. Scientists are still not sure whether** ***Mononykus*** **was a bird or a dinosaur.**

Sprinters

Toward the end of the Age of Dinosaurs, some of the meat-eaters became more and more birdlike. Some big ones, the ornithomimids, looked like ostriches.

Struthiomimus
Struthiomimus **was an ornithomimid the size of a present-day ostrich. It may also have been one of the fastest. Some scientists think that it could run as fast as 50 miles (80 kilometers) an hour.**

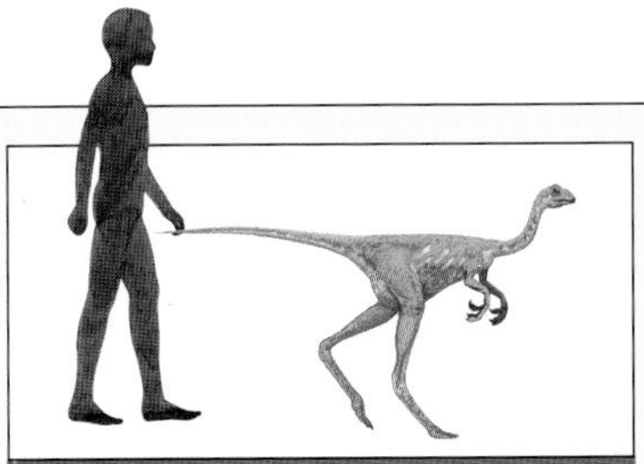

FACTS AND FIGURES

Avimimus

(AH-vee-MIM-mus)

Meaning of Name: "Bird mimic"–thought to look like a bird

Classification: Raptor

Size, Weight: 5 feet ($1\frac{1}{2}$ meters), 30 pounds (14 kilograms)

Time: Late Cretaceous, 85 to 75 million years ago

Place: Mongolia

Food: Unknown

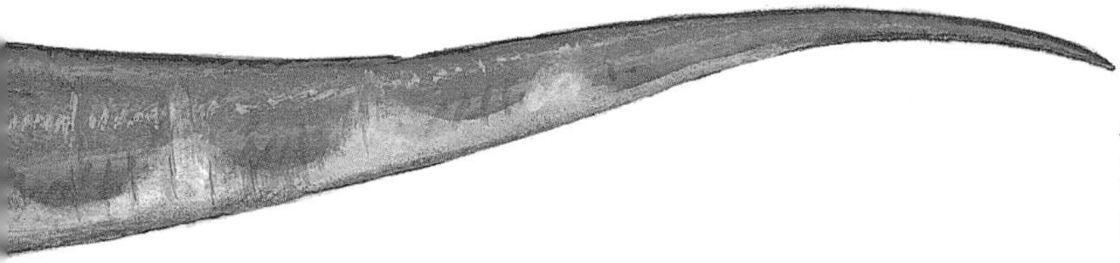

Avimimus

Some scientists think *Avimimus* might have been covered with feathers because its skeleton is so similar to that of a bird. The feathers would not have been used for flying. Instead, they may have helped to keep the animal warm.

FACTS AND FIGURES

Struthiomimus

(STROO-thee-o-MIM-mus)

Meaning of Name: "Ostrich mimic"–thought to look like an ostrich

Classification: Raptor

Size, Weight: 13 feet (4 meters) long, 300 pounds (136 kilograms)

Time: Late Cretaceous, 76 to 68 million years ago

Place: Alberta

Food: Small animals, insects, eggs, maybe fruit

Although ornithomimids were raptors—a Latin word meaning "robber"—they may have eaten fruits and tender plants as well as meat. This is similar to the way bears and pandas today are related to the meat-eating cats and dogs.

Smart for Its Age

Troodon

Troodon **must have been a good hunter. It had large eyes, keen hearing, and hands that could grasp. It also had agile legs and a long tail, for balance. These would have helped it make quick turns when chasing fast prey.**

FACTS AND FIGURES

Troodon

(TROH-o-don)

Meaning of Name: "Tearing tooth"—its sharp teeth were the first parts to be found

Classification: Raptor

Size, Weight: 6 feet (2 meters) long, 30 pounds (14 kilograms)

Time: Late Cretaceous, 76 to 70 million years ago

Place: Western North America

Food: Meat, particularly small animals

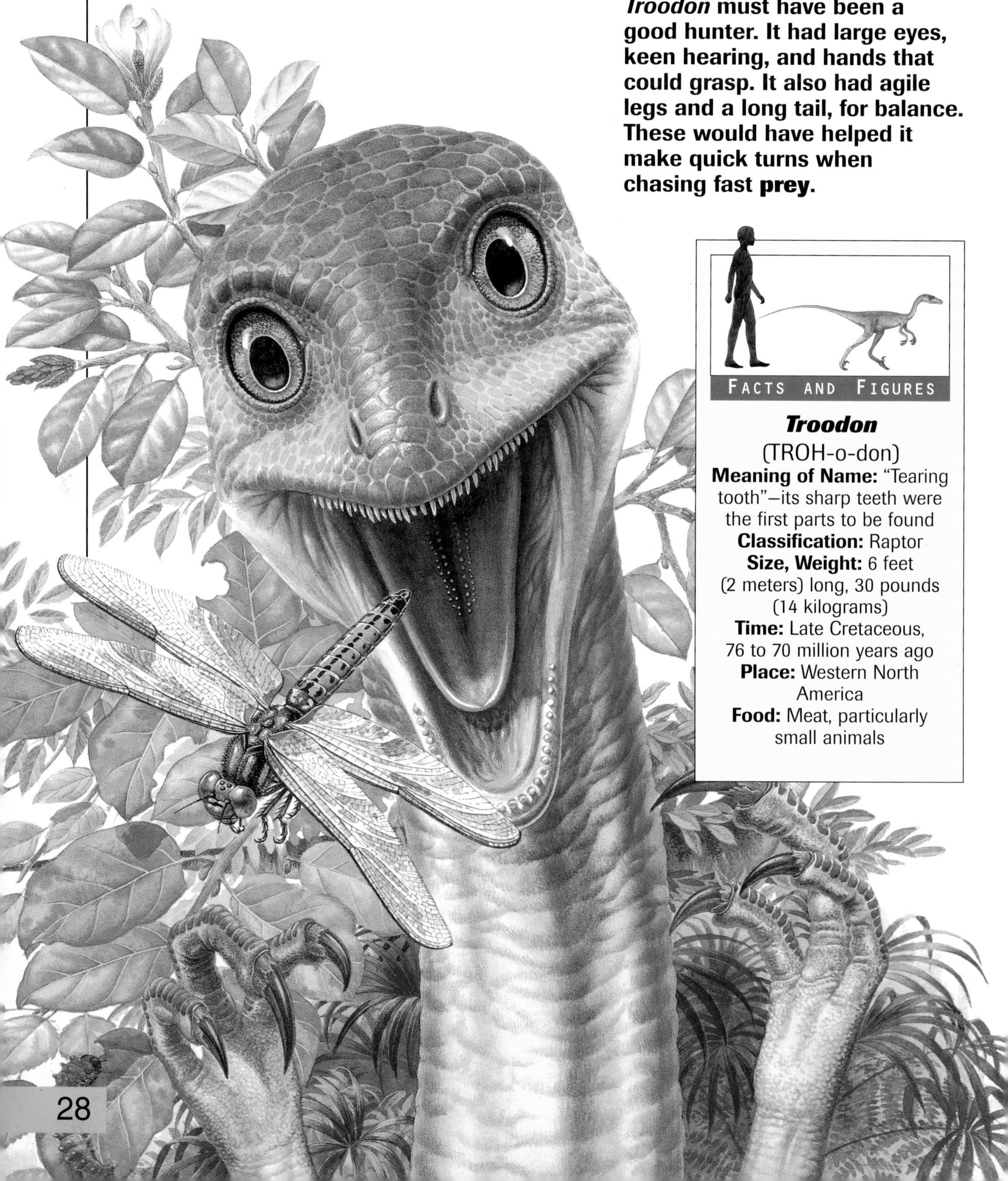

We often think of dinosaurs as being slow, stupid animals. But some dinosaurs, such as *Troodon*, had big brains in proportion to body size. That does not make them very bright compared with humans, but it makes them much brighter than any other **reptile** we know.

Oviraptor
The first *Oviraptor* skeleton was found in a nest of dinosaur eggs. Scientists thought that it was robbing the nest, and named it *Oviraptor*, or "egg thief," but now we know that the nest was its own.

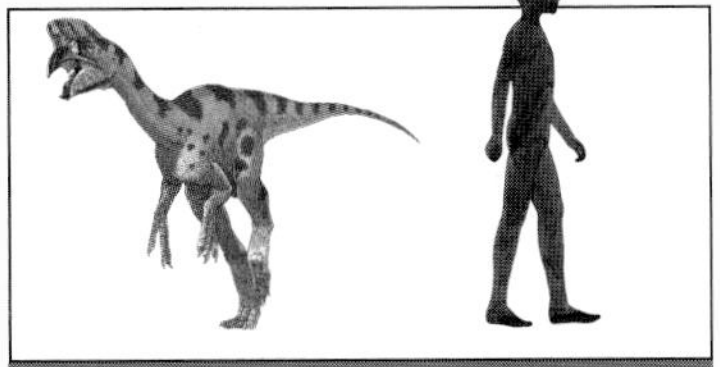

FACTS AND FIGURES

Oviraptor

(O-vih-RAP-tur)

Meaning of Name: "Egg thief"–thought to have been stealing eggs

Classification: Raptor

Size, Weight: 6 feet (2 meters) long, 50–100 pounds (23–45 kilograms)

Time: Late Cretaceous, 88 to 70 million years ago

Place: Mongolia

Food: Meat, possibly fruits, insects, shellfish, and grubs

Terrible Reptile

For killing power, *Tyrannosaurus* was unrivaled among dinosaurs. When hunting, it probably hid among the shadows of the forests until its prey approached. Then suddenly it charged. Pushing with its massive legs, it thrust itself forward. It dropped its jaw, opening its mouth and exposing its huge teeth. It swept down its great jaws, tearing off strips of flesh. Its prey died of shock and loss of blood.

***Tyrannosaurus*'s huge head, strong saw-like teeth, and little arms make it the best-known and most recognizable of all dinosaurs.**

Muscle and Bone

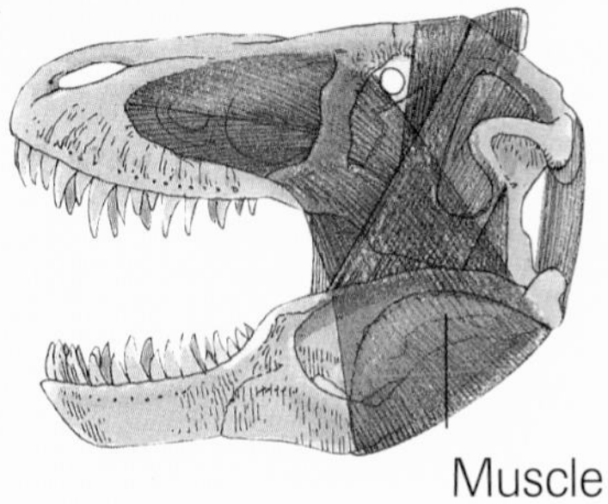

This *Tyrannosaurus* skull shows thick pointed teeth, each as long as a steak knife. The hinged jaws were moved by a wide band of muscle, which helped to open the mouth wide.

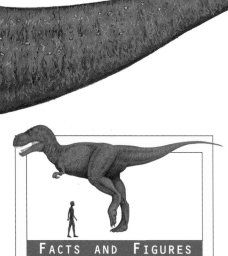

Facts and Figures

Tyrannosaurus

(tie-RAN-uh-SAW-rus)

Meaning of Name: "Tyrant lizard"

Classification: Tyrannosaur

Size, Weight: 38 feet ($11\frac{1}{2}$ meters) long, 6 tons (5,400 kilograms)

Time: End of the Cretaceous, 68 to 65 million years ago

Place: North America

Food: Other dinosaurs, perhaps including those already dead

For ninety years we thought *Tyrannosaurus* was the biggest meat-eating dinosaur. But now we are finding the remains of even bigger meat-eaters.

Big and Fierce

In recent years, the remains of huge meat-eating dinosaurs have been found all over the world. We used to think that *Tyrannosaurus* was the biggest and that giant **carnivores** like this lived only in North America. Now we are finding even bigger meat-eaters in South America and in Africa.

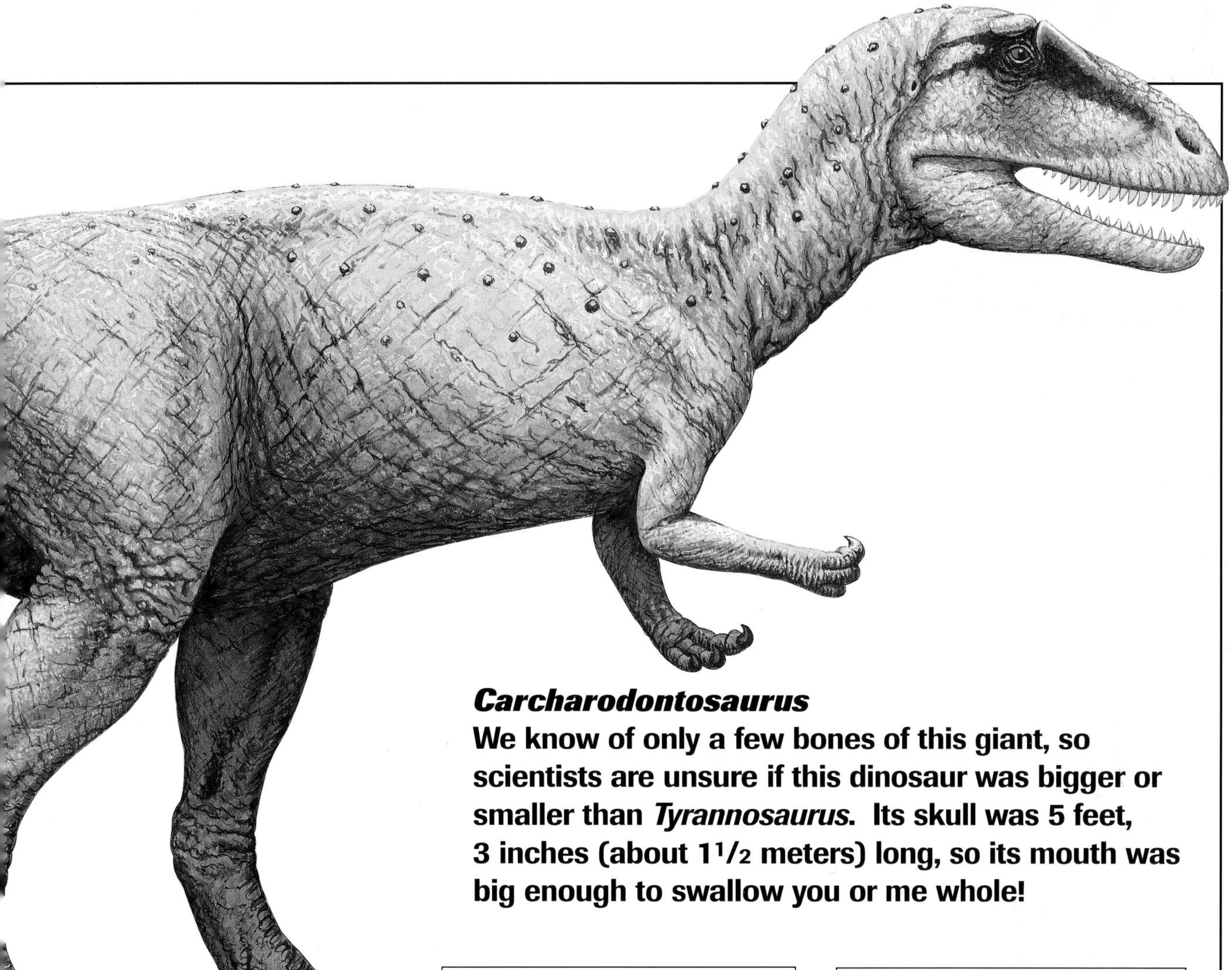

Carcharodontosaurus
We know of only a few bones of this giant, so scientists are unsure if this dinosaur was bigger or smaller than *Tyrannosaurus*. Its skull was 5 feet, 3 inches (about $1\frac{1}{2}$ meters) long, so its mouth was big enough to swallow you or me whole!

Giganotosaurus
In 1995, the skeleton of *Giganotosaurus* was found in South America. It was even longer than that of *Tyrannosaurus.* It was not a close relative, however. It was more closely related to *Allosaurus* of the Jurassic Period.

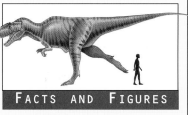

FACTS AND FIGURES

Giganotosaurus
(JIH-ga-NO-toe-SAW-rus)

Meaning of Name: "Gigantic southern lizard"–found in the Southern Hemisphere
Classification: Allosaur
Size, Weight: 42 feet (13 meters) long, 8 tons (7 tonnes)
Time: Beginning of the Late Cretaceous, 90 million years ago
Place: Argentina
Food: Other dinosaurs

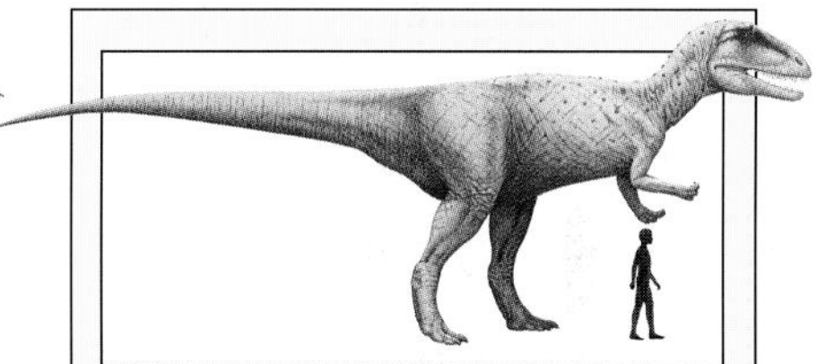

FACTS AND FIGURES

Carcharodontosaurus
(car-CARE-oh-DON-tuh-SAW-rus)

Meaning of Name: "Great white shark lizard"–because of its big, shark-like teeth
Classification: Allosaur
Size, Weight: 35–43 feet ($10\frac{1}{2}$-13 meters) long, up to 8 tons (7 tonnes)
Time: Beginning of the Late Cretaceous, 97 to 90 million years ago
Place: North Africa
Food: Other dinosaurs

Long-Necked Plant-Eaters

The biggest dinosaurs of all were the long-necked plant-eaters, or **sauropods**. All kinds of sauropods lived together. Some ate from low-growing **vegetation**. Others had long necks and fed on the leaves at the tops of trees.

Nearly 170 million years ago in central China, herds of plant-eating dinosaurs munch their way through a lush forest by the side of a stream. A pterosaur flies overhead.

KEY
1 *Omeisaurus*
2 *Shunosaurus*

Range of Sizes

The biggest animals that ever walked the Earth were the long-necked plant-eaters. They belonged to a group called the **sauropods**, which means "lizard-footed." Sauropods were named by early **paleontologists**, who noted that the bones of their feet were similar to those of a lizard. The sauropods were more closely related to the meat-eating **theropods** than they were to other plant-eating dinosaurs.

BABY MUSSAURUS

The smallest dinosaur skeleton found was about the size of a songbird's. It was called *Mussaurus*, or "mouse lizard," and it was actually the skeleton of a baby. The adult dinosaur would have been about 10 feet (3 meters) long.

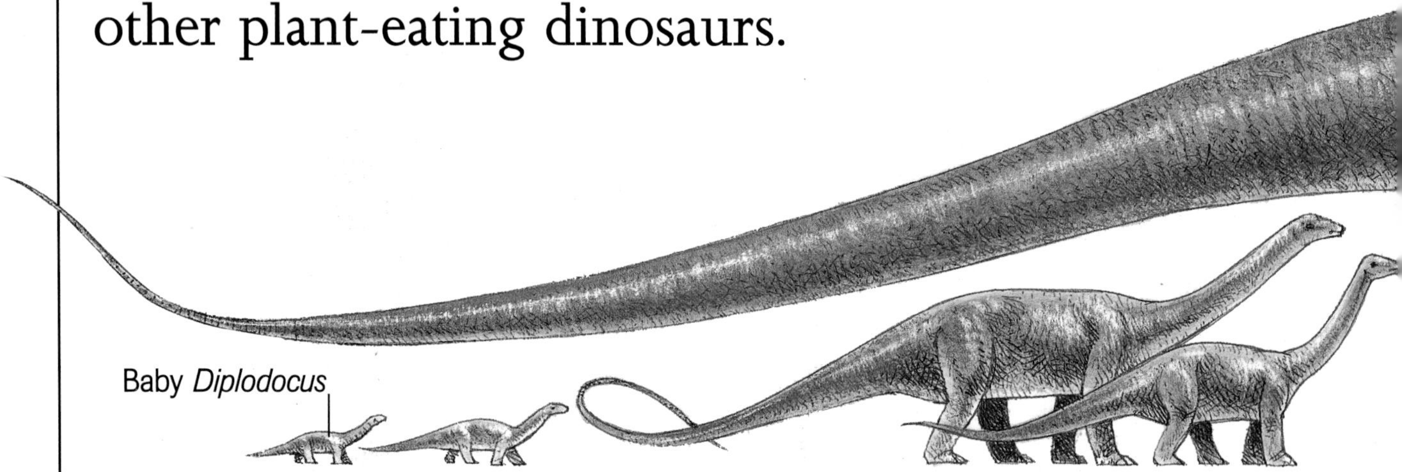

Dinosaur Babies
Even though sauropods grew quite large, their babies were small.

If the babies were very large, they would not have been able to fit into an egg.

Some scientists think that dinosaurs grew fast, reaching their large size in less than 20 years.

Food Pyramid
Big animals need much more food than small animals do. That is why, in dinosaur times, a particular area would have supported many thousands of tiny insects and amphibians (including frogs), a few hundred small reptiles and mammals, fifty or so small dinosaurs, but only one really big dinosaur. To find enough food for its massive body, *Tyrannosaurus* probably had to roam over a large area.

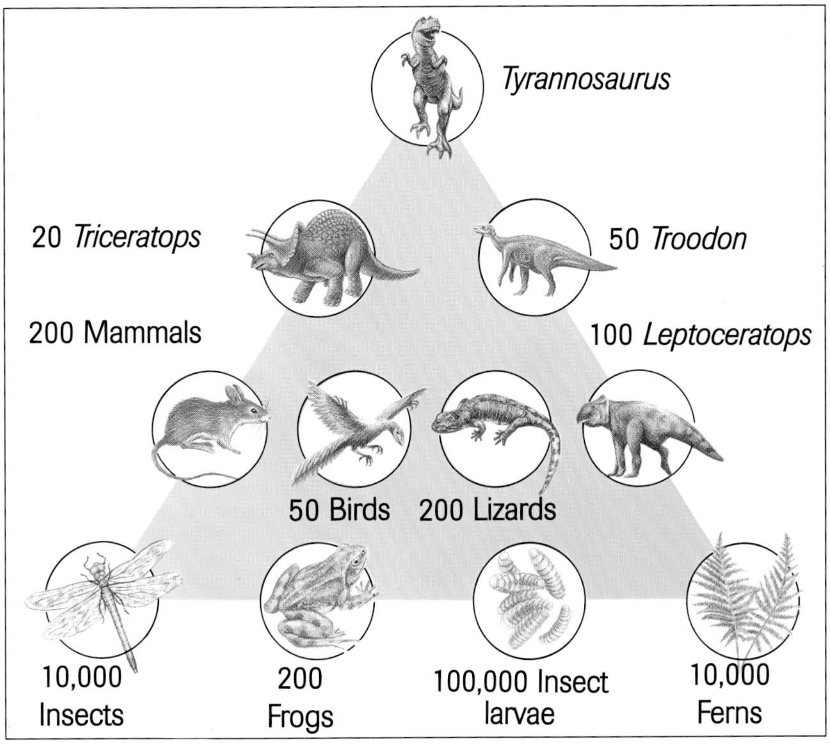

Diplodocus
Look at the size of this sauropod compared with the size of an elephant and a human being!

It is called *Diplodocus*, and when it was alive, it would have been 90 feet (27 meters) long.

Some sauropods were even bigger.

Inside a Giant

The insides of a plant-eating animal are quite different from the insides of a meat-eater. Plants are more difficult to **digest** than meat, so the stomach and **intestines** of a plant-eater need to be large. This means that a plant-eater has a bigger body than a meat-eater.

Food Requirements
A big sauropod, such as *Seismosaurus*, spent most of its time eating to fuel its massive body. As it digested its food, it also dropped dung. Every day it must have eaten more than 500 pounds (227 kilograms) of food and dropped hundreds of pounds of dung.

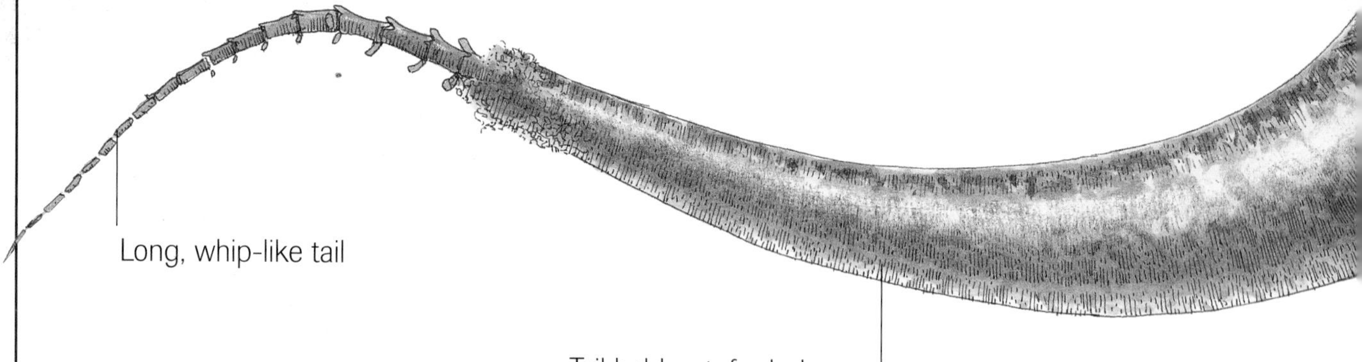

Stomach Stones

Big plant-eaters sometimes swallowed stones, or gastroliths, to help them digest their food. These stomach stones helped to grind and break up the plant food in the stomach so that it could be digested more easily.

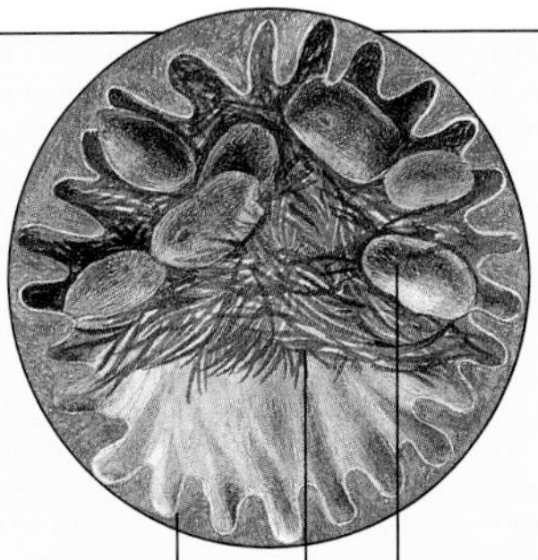

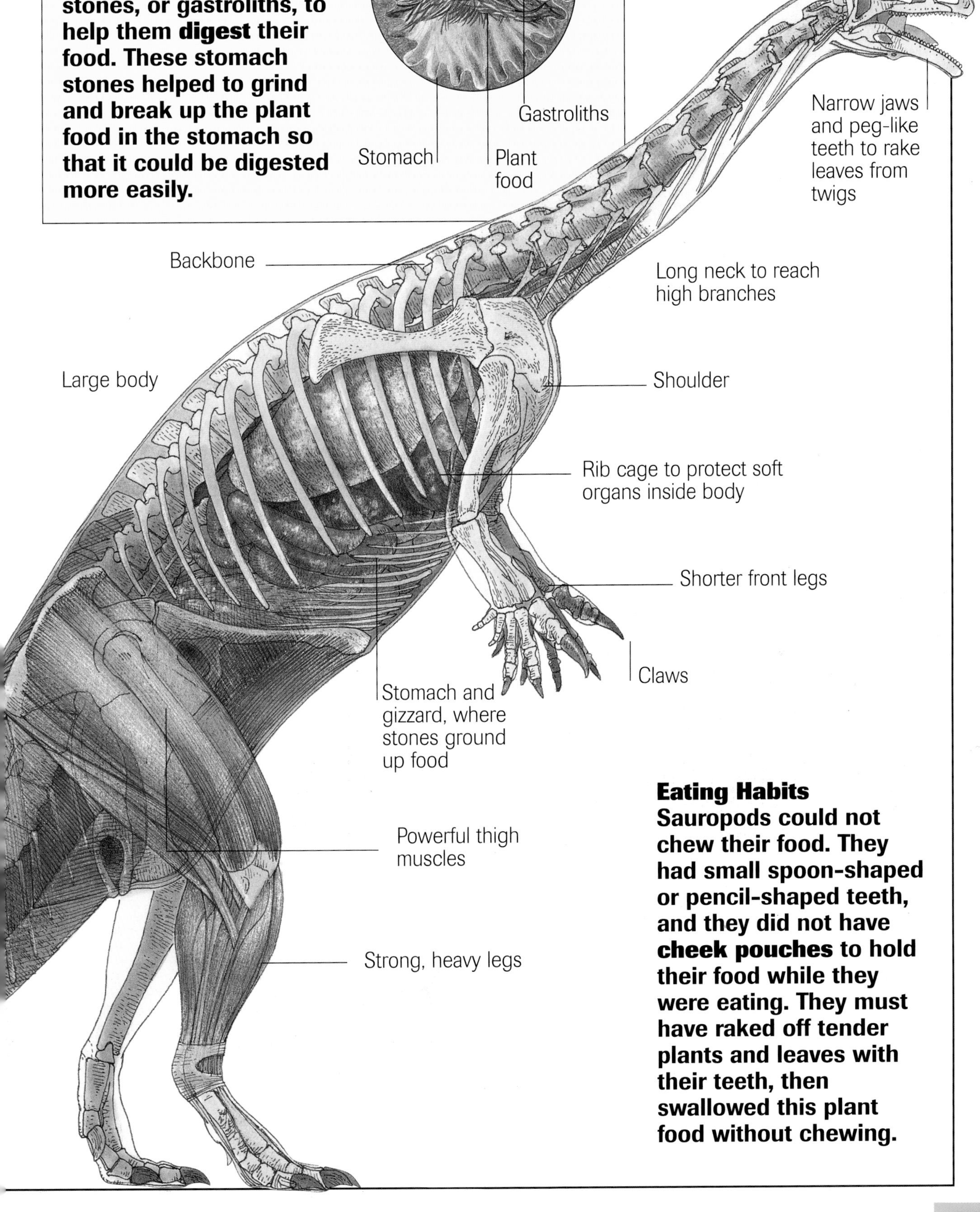

Eating Habits

Sauropods could not chew their food. They had small spoon-shaped or pencil-shaped teeth, and they did not have cheek pouches to hold their food while they were eating. They must have raked off tender plants and leaves with their teeth, then swallowed this plant food without chewing.

Vulnerable in Death

Plants use the energy of sunlight to make their own food. Plant-eaters eat that food, and meat-eaters eat the plant-eaters. This "food chain" is at work today, just as it was at the time of the dinosaurs.

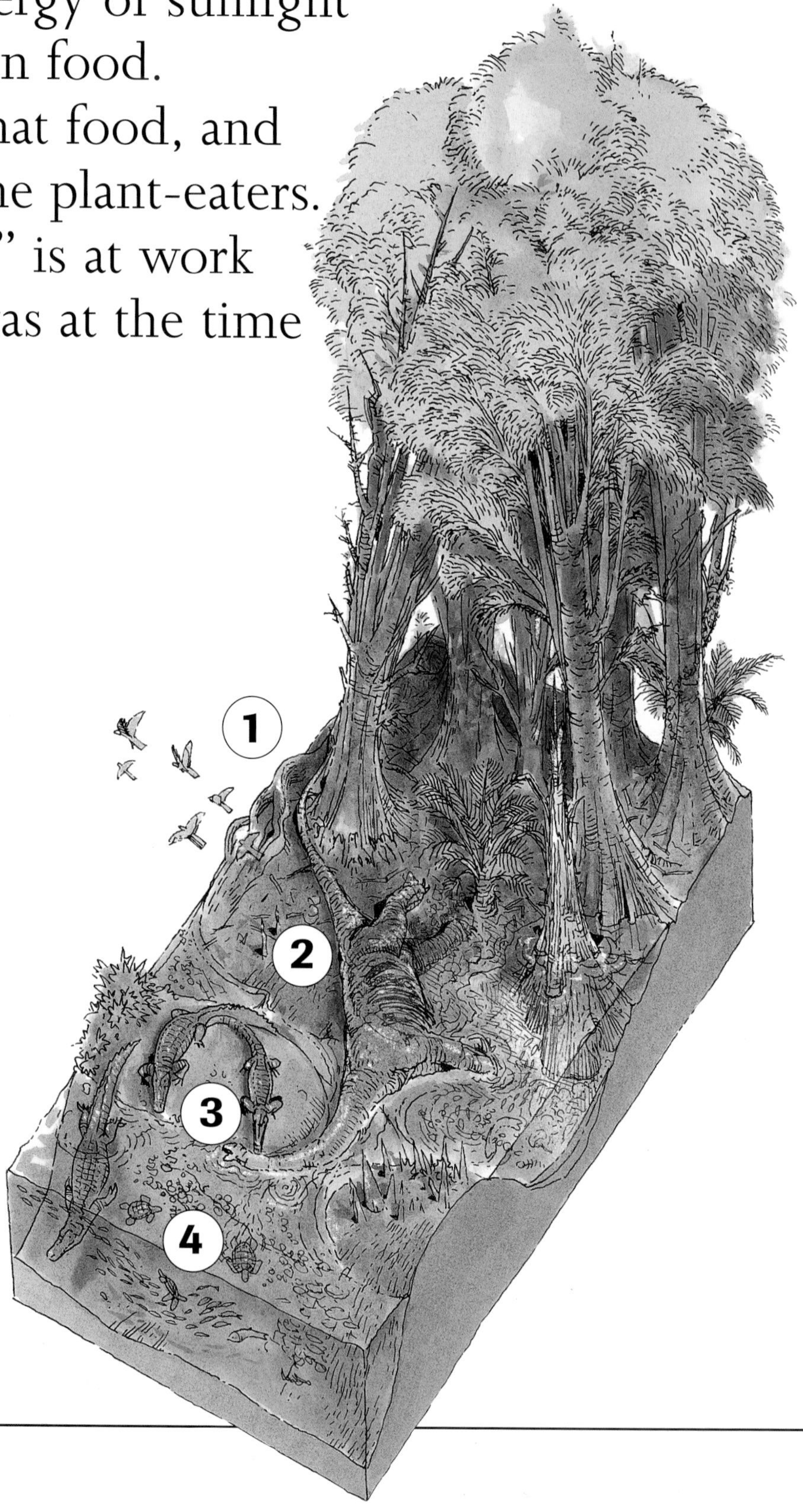

Food for the Many
A dead long-necked plant-eater was good food for all kinds of animals. The body of one of these giants lying by the side of a river would have been eaten by birds, crocodiles, fish, and turtles. What these animals left behind would have been eaten by insects and tiny creatures living in the water, and rotted away by bacteria.

KEY
1 Birds
2 Dead long-necked plant-eater
3 Crocodiles
4 Turtles

Afrovenator
Big meat-eaters, such as *Afrovenator*, may have spent much of their time hunting and killing their own food, but they would not have passed up the chance of eating any dead dinosaur that they found.

A big plant-eater, such as *Camarasaurus*, would be difficult to kill. However, once it had been killed or had died of natural causes, it would have provided a mountain of meat for all kinds of animals.

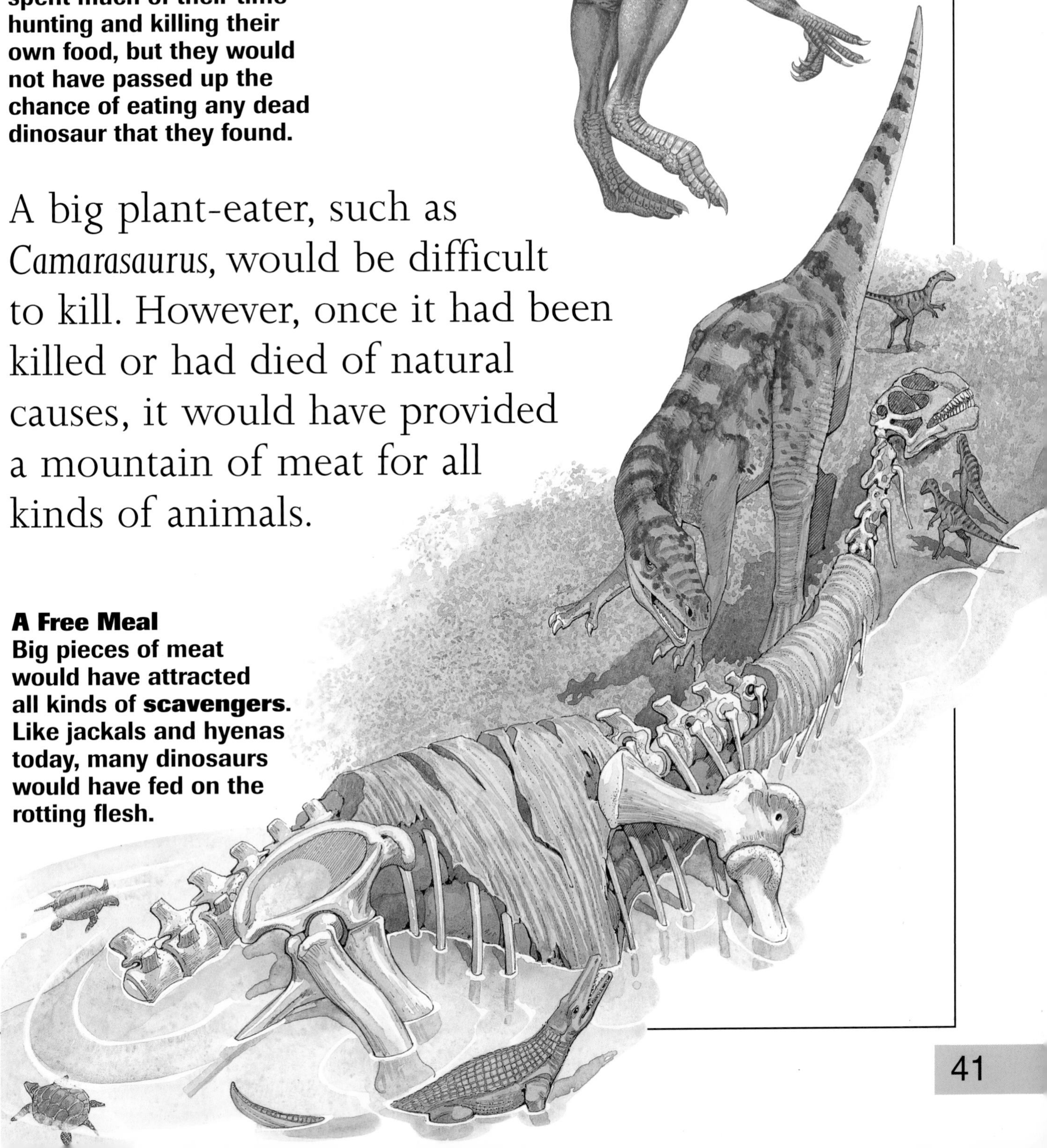

A Free Meal
Big pieces of meat would have attracted all kinds of scavengers. Like jackals and hyenas today, many dinosaurs would have fed on the rotting flesh.

Early Biggies

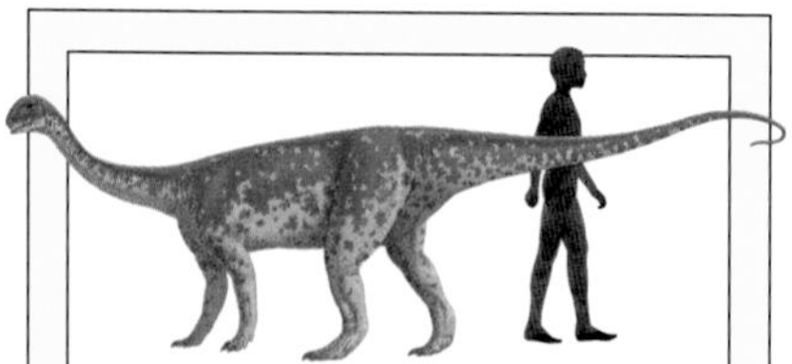

FACTS AND FIGURES

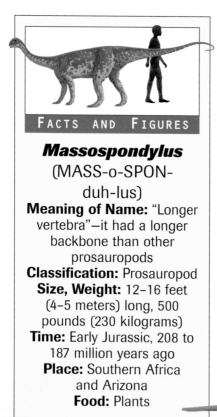

Massospondylus
(MASS-o-SPON-duh-lus)
Meaning of Name: "Longer vertebra"—it had a longer backbone than other prosauropods
Classification: Prosauropod
Size, Weight: 12–16 feet (4–5 meters) long, 500 pounds (230 kilograms)
Time: Early Jurassic, 208 to 187 million years ago
Place: Southern Africa and Arizona
Food: Plants

The prosauropods were the first of the really big plant-eating dinosaurs. Just as the later **sauropods**, they each had a small head carried at the end of a long neck. Most of the time they stood on all four legs, but they could rear up on their hind legs for short periods of time.

Massospondylus
***Massospondylus* was a medium-sized prosauropod. It had large eyes and large nostrils, so it must have had good eyesight and a keen sense of smell.**

FACTS AND FIGURES

Plateosaurus
(PLAT-ee-o-SAW-rus)
Meaning of Name: "Broad lizard"—had a wide, broad body
Classification: Prosauropod, a group that came before the true sauropods
Size, Weight: 20–26 feet (6–8 meters) long, 2,000–4,000 pounds (900–1,800 kilograms)
Time: Late Triassic, 222 to 208 million years ago
Place: Greenland, Germany, France, and Switzerland
Food: Plants

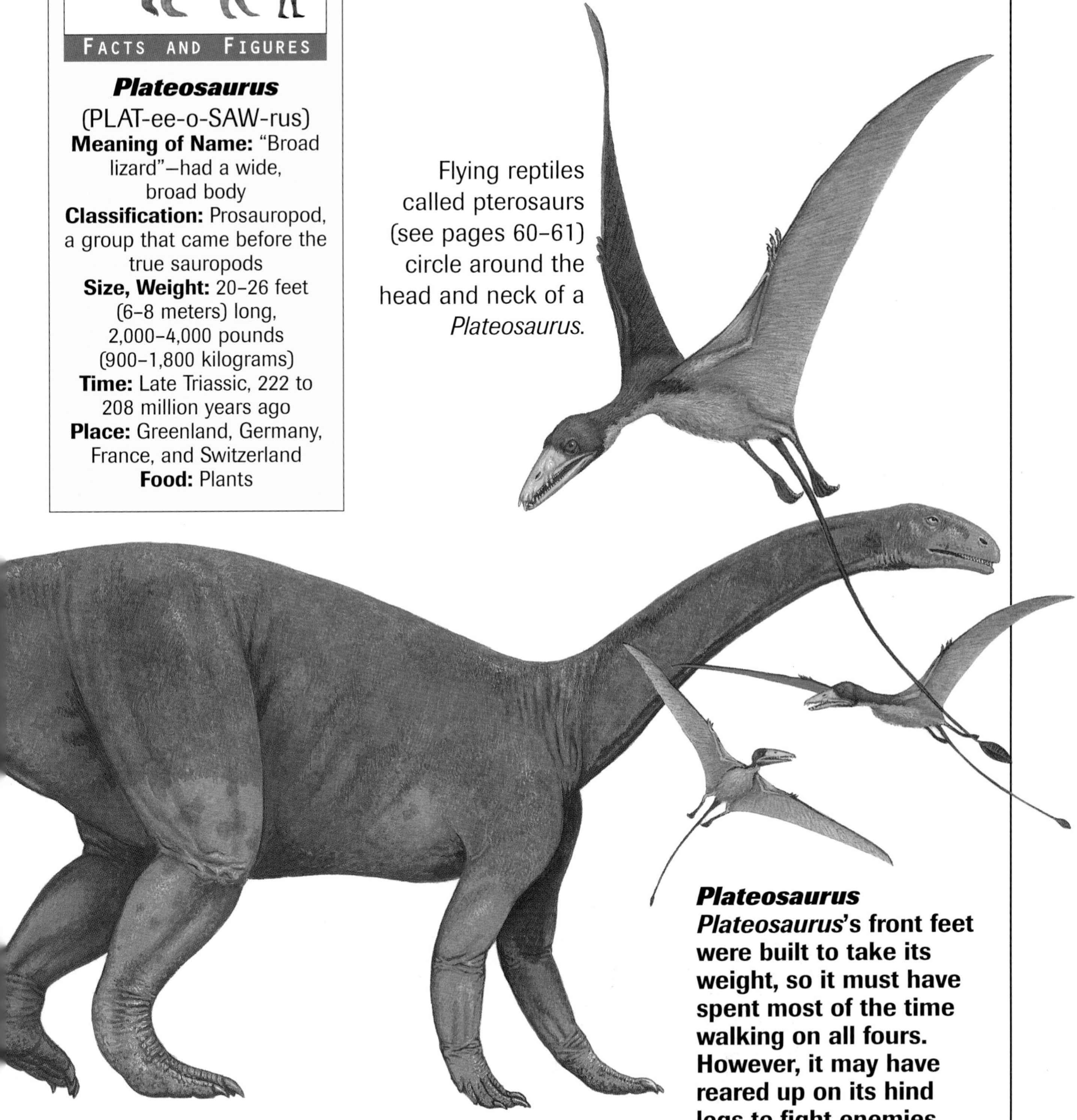

Flying reptiles called pterosaurs (see pages 60–61) circle around the head and neck of a *Plateosaurus*.

Plateosaurus
***Plateosaurus*'s front feet were built to take its weight, so it must have spent most of the time walking on all fours. However, it may have reared up on its hind legs to fight enemies or to pull down vegetation with its thumb claws.**

Going for Height

There were many kinds of plants in the **Jurassic** Period, from low-growing **ferns** and **horsetails** to giant **conifer trees** and **tree ferns**. It is not surprising, therefore, that plant-eating dinosaurs **evolved** in different ways to eat these different supplies of food. Some **herbivores** fed on plants growing close to the ground. Others had long necks and could eat shoots and leaves at the tops of trees.

Brachiosaurus
Brachiosaurus had long front legs that raised its shoulders high above the ground. From these high shoulders, *Brachiosaurus* could stretch its neck into the treetops, as a modern-day giraffe does, and **browse** on tender shoots.

Different sizes and neck lengths allowed prosauropods and sauropods to eat different sources of food.

KEY
1 ***Plateosaurus***
2 ***Diplodocus***
3 ***Supersaurus***
4 ***Brachiosaurus***
5 ***Seismosaurus***

FACTS AND FIGURES

Brachiosaurus

(BRACK-ee-o-SAW-rus)
Meaning of Name: "Arm lizard"—its front legs were longer than its back legs
Classification: Sauropod
Size, Weight: 75 feet (23 meters) long, 40 feet (12 meters) to raised head, 80 tons (73 tonnes)
Time: Late Jurassic, 156 to 145 million years ago
Place: Colorado, and Tanzania, East Africa
Food: Leaves

Going to Extremes

A big animal is harder to kill than a small animal. In a place and a time when there were vicious meat-eaters, such as *Allosaurus* and *Ceratosaurus*, a large animal would have been safer than a smaller one. The long-necked plant-eaters, or **sauropods**, would have had little to fear, even from the biggest meat-eaters.

FACTS AND FIGURES

Seismosaurus
(SIZE-mo-SAW-rus)
Meaning of Name: "Earthquake lizard"—it was so big!
Classification: Sauropod
Size, Weight: 120–150 feet (37–45 meters) long, 40 tons (36 tonnes)

Time: Late Jurassic, 156 to 145 million years ago
Place: New Mexico
Food: Leaves

Seismosaurus
Seismosaurus **was discovered in 1985. Scientists worked out that it was half the length of a football field. The skeleton was firmly buried in hard rock, and it took 10 years to dig it out.**

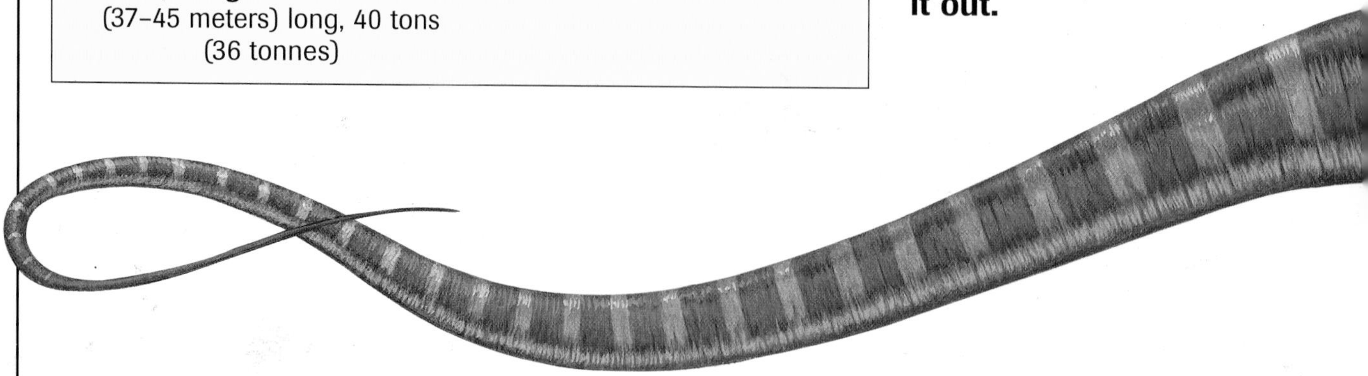

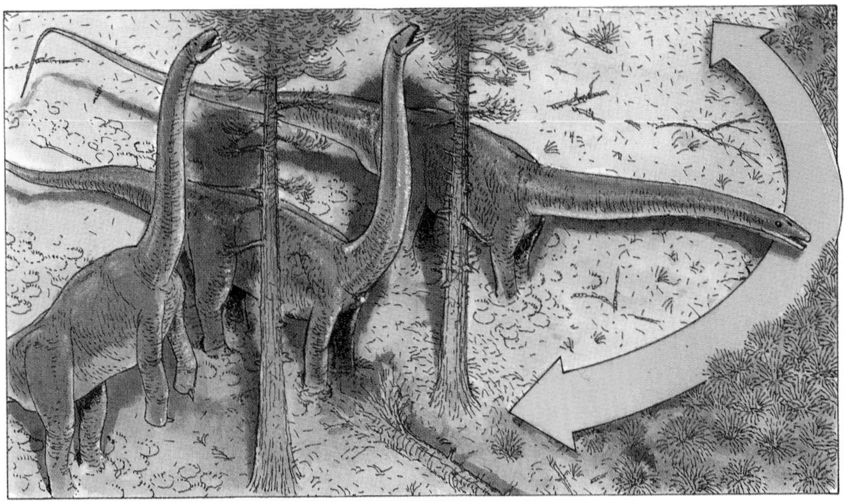

Sweeping Necks
It may have been hard for *Seismosaurus* to keep its giraffe-like neck raised for long periods of time. Perhaps it used its neck like the flexible hose on a vacuum cleaner, sweeping its head from side to side along the ground or low-lying **vegetation.**

Seismosaurus was a giant among sauropods. It probably had to eat all its waking hours to get the energy it needed. It must have eaten more than an elephant, which each day eats as much as 500 pounds (240 kilograms) of plant material.

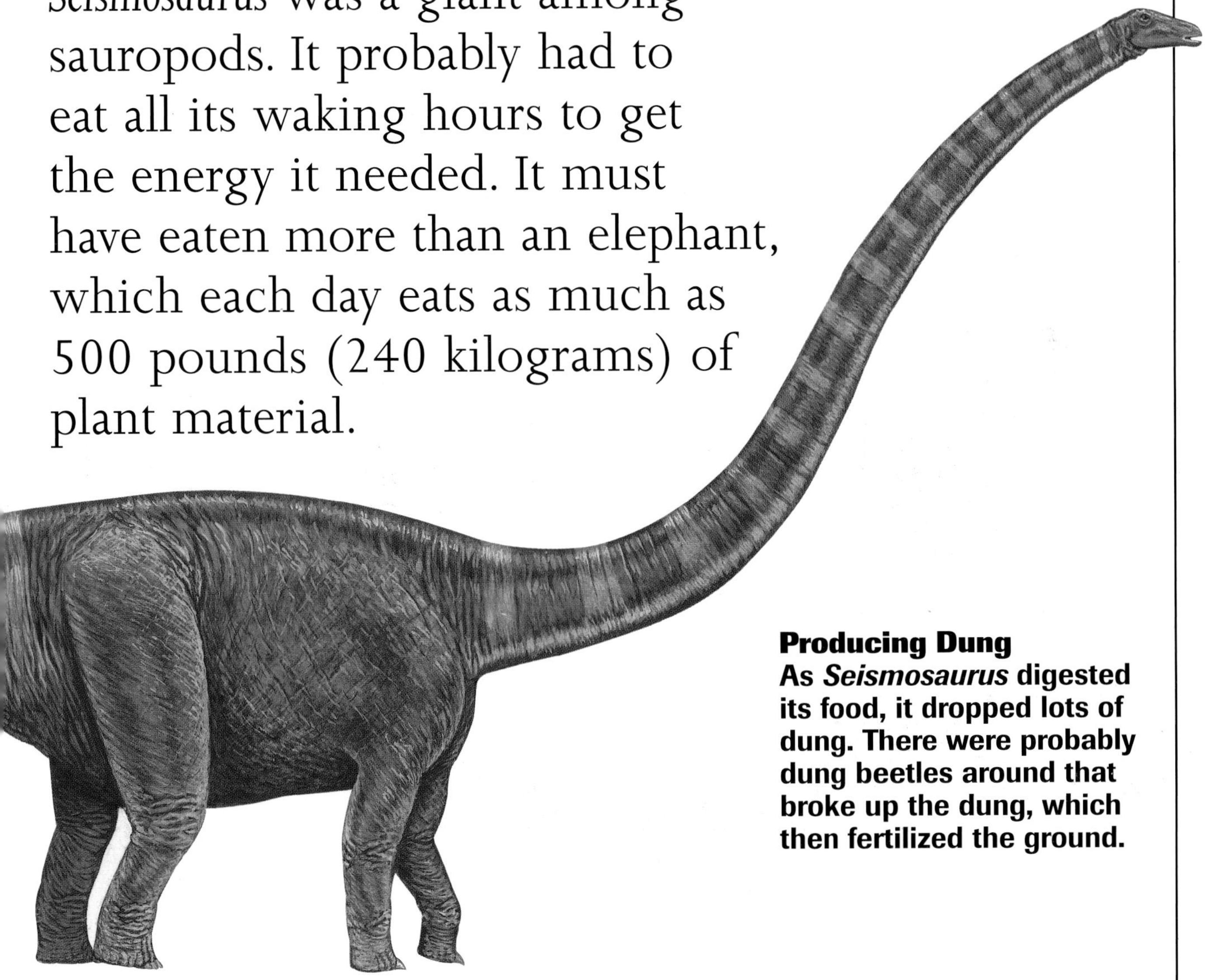

Producing Dung
As *Seismosaurus* digested its food, it dropped lots of dung. There were probably dung beetles around that broke up the dung, which then fertilized the ground.

Chinese Giants

In the early days of dinosaur hunting, nearly all **sauropod** skeletons were found in North America. However, during the last 50 years, many long-necks have been found in central China. Their skeletons are well preserved and give us a good picture of what the animals looked like when they were alive.

Shunosaurus
Shunosaurus **is the only sauropod we know with a club at the end of its tail. It may have used the club like a weapon, to fight off predators.**

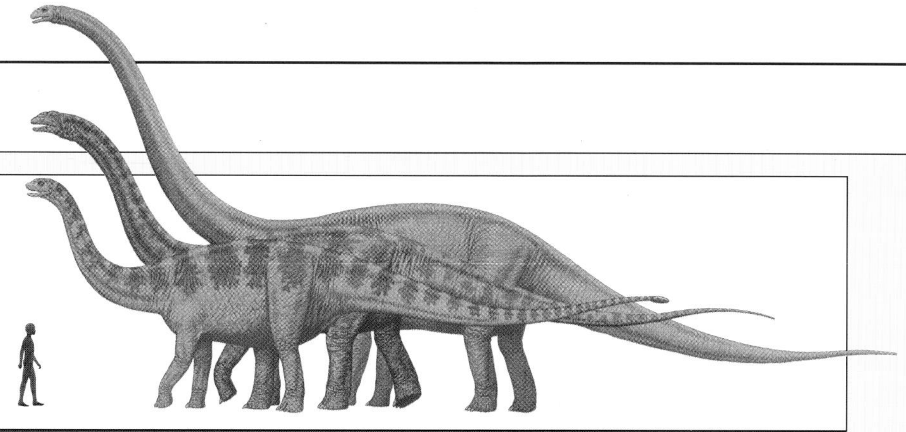

FACTS AND FIGURES

Omeisaurus
(O-mee-SAW-rus)
Meaning of Name: "Sacred mountain lizard"—after a mountain near the spot where it was found
Classification: Sauropod
Size, Weight: 65 feet (20 meters) long, 20 tons (18 tonnes)
Time: Late Jurassic, 165 to 145 million years ago
Place: China
Food: Leaves

Datousaurus
(DAT-oo-SAW-rus)
Meaning of Name: "Lizard from Datou"—found in Datou Province, China
Classification: Sauropod
Size, Weight: 50 feet (15 meters) long, 20 tons (18 tonnes)
Time: Middle Jurassic, 170 to 163 million years ago
Place: China
Food: Leaves

Shunosaurus
(SHOO-no-SAW-rus)
Meaning of Name: "Lizard from Shou"—the old name for Sichuan Province, China
Classification: Sauropod
Size, Weight: 40 feet (12 metres) long, 10 tons (9 tonnes)
Time: Middle Jurassic, 175 to 163 million years ago
Place: China
Food: Leaves

Omeisaurus
Many skeletons of _Omeisaurus_ were found in the same place, showing that the animals traveled in herds, as elephants do today.

Datousaurus
This dinosaur was closely related to _Omeisaurus,_ which may have been the ancestor of the later diplodocids—the long, low sauropods.

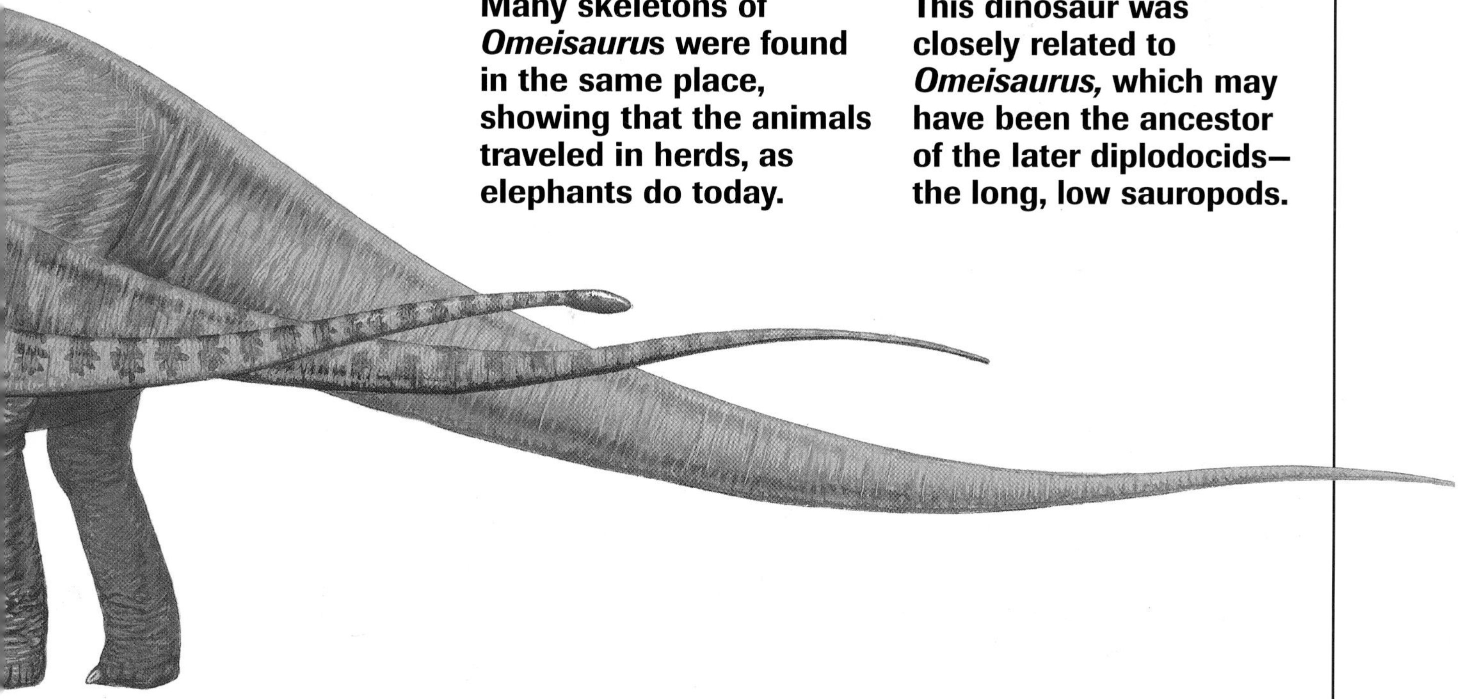

Armored Long-Necks

Most of the **sauropods** lived in the **Jurassic** Period. However, one group, the titanosaurs, did not appear until the end of the Jurassic and survived until the end of the **Cretaceous** Period.

In Madagascar as long ago as 1896, a French **paleontologist** found a skeleton of a titanosaur, named *Titanosaurus*, that had a piece of armor alongside it.

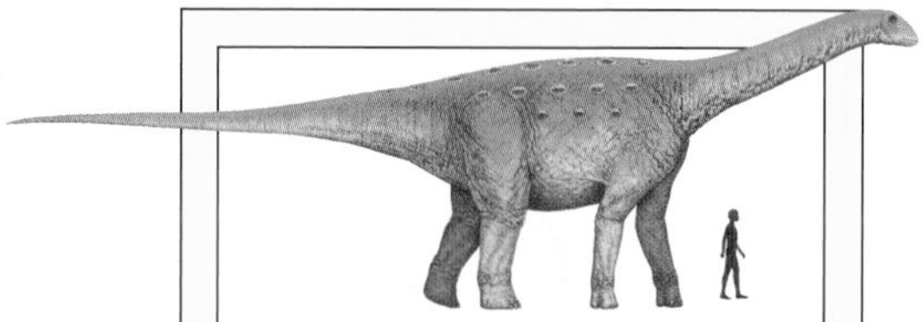

FACTS AND FIGURES

Titanosaurus
(tie-TAN-o-SAW-rus)
Meaning of Name: "Huge lizard"
Classification: Titanosaur
Size, Weight: 30–60 feet (9–18 meters) long, 3–15 tons (3–14 tonnes)
Time: Late Cretaceous, 90 to 65 million years ago
Place: India, Argentina, and Madagascar
Food: Plants

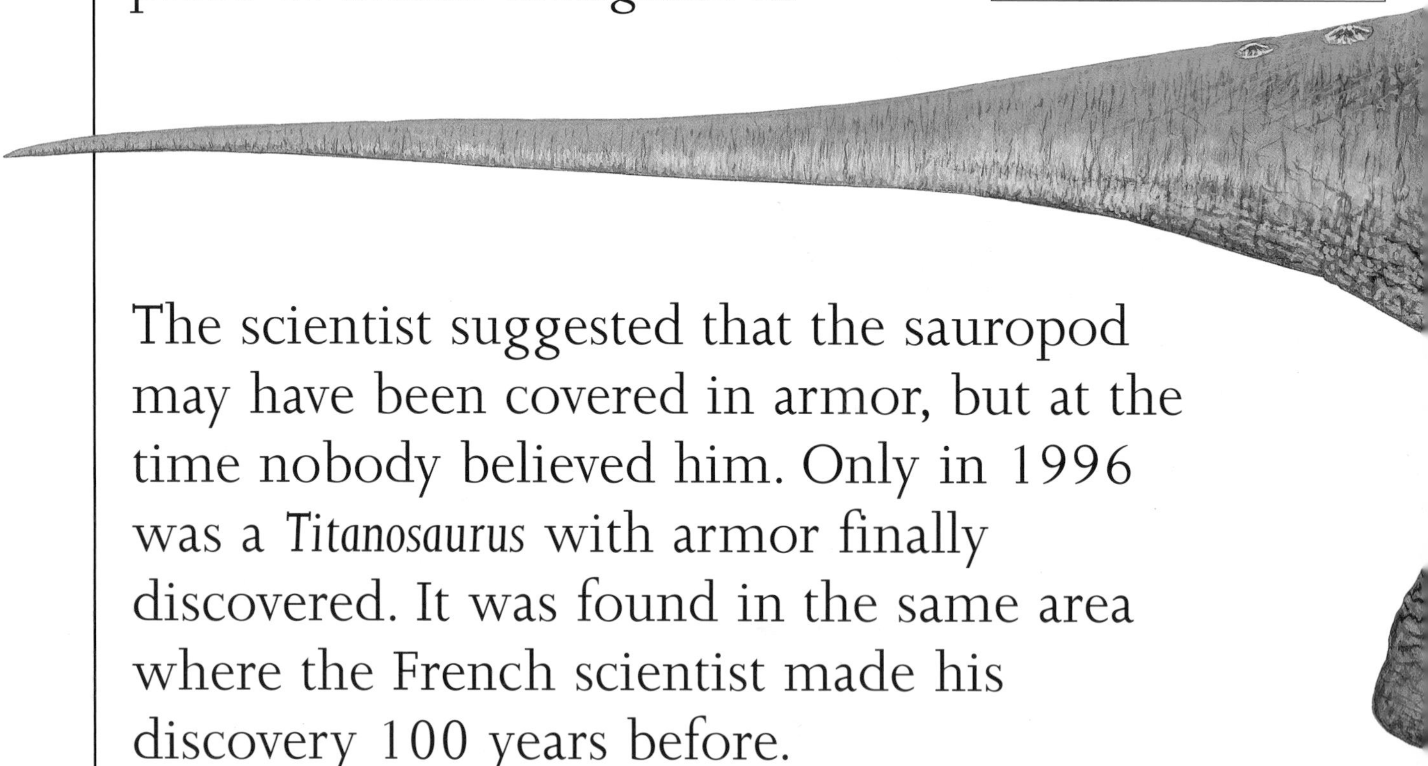

The scientist suggested that the sauropod may have been covered in armor, but at the time nobody believed him. Only in 1996 was a *Titanosaurus* with armor finally discovered. It was found in the same area where the French scientist made his discovery 100 years before.

STAYING APART

At the end of the Cretaceous Period the two-footed plant-eaters had become more common in the northern part of the world than the sauropods. It may be that the two-footed plant-eaters fed in the forests of flowering trees while the titanosaurs stayed in the coniferous and fern forests.

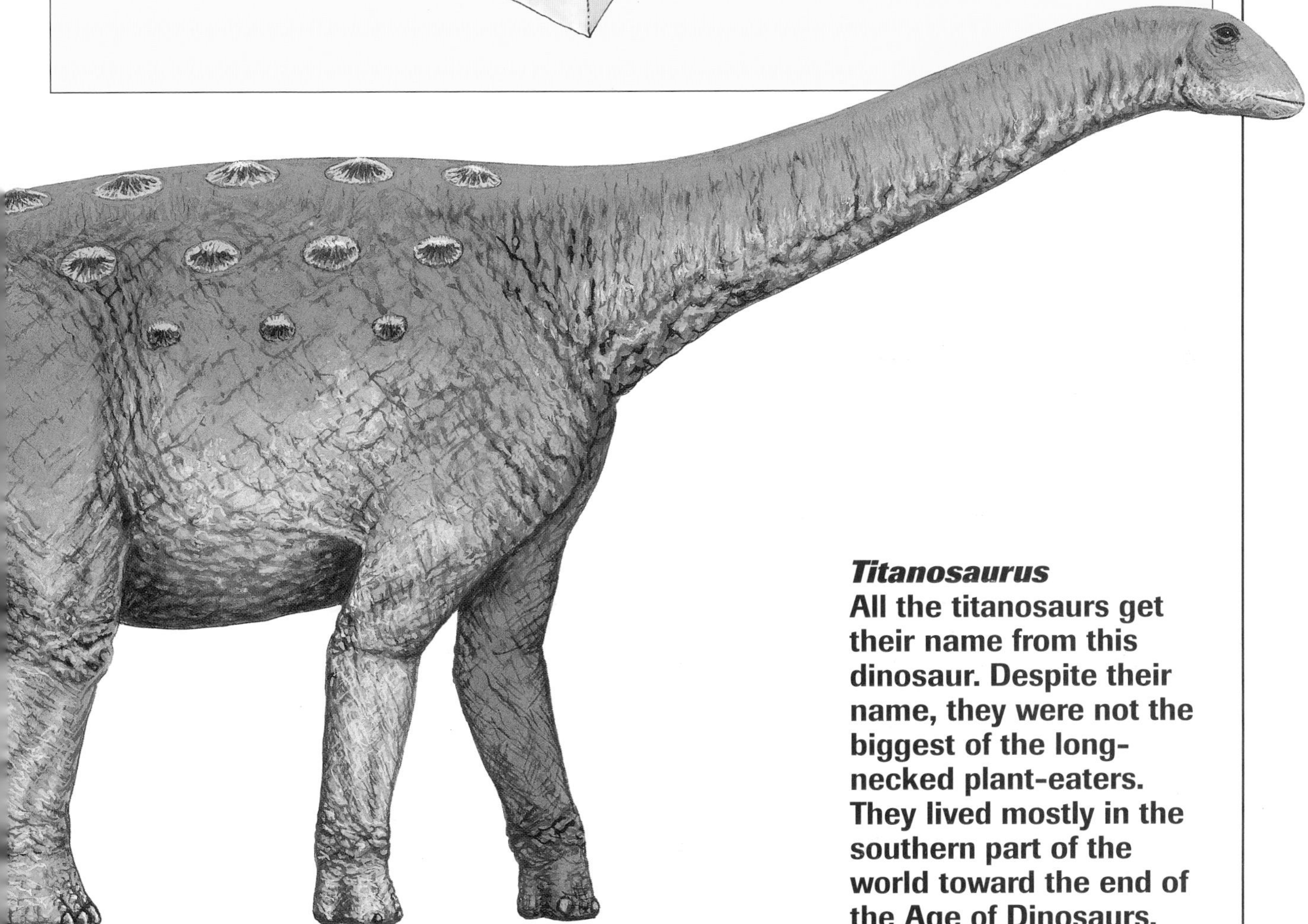

Titanosaurus

All the titanosaurs get their name from this dinosaur. Despite their name, they were not the biggest of the long-necked plant-eaters. They lived mostly in the southern part of the world toward the end of the Age of Dinosaurs.

Plates with Ridges

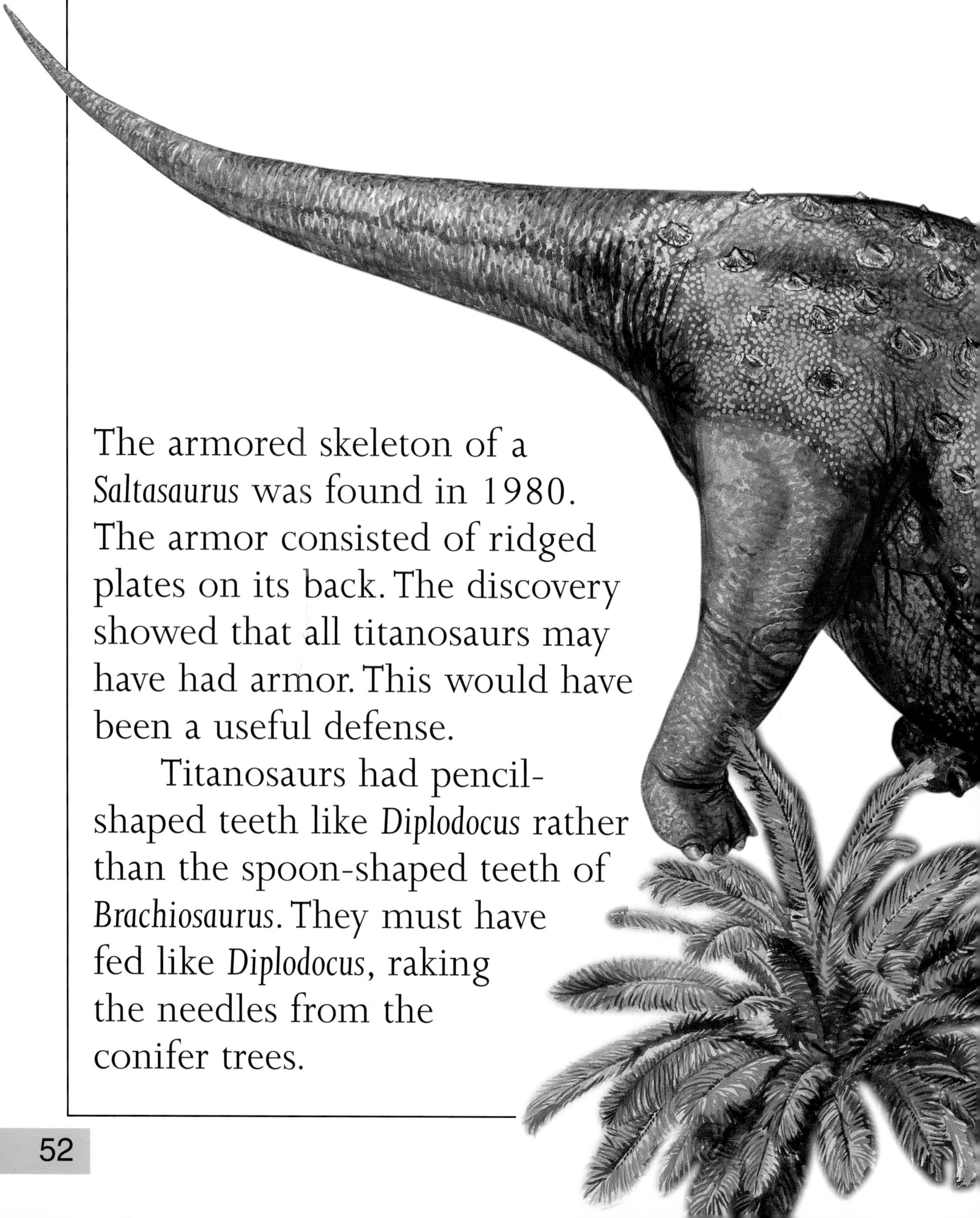

The armored skeleton of a *Saltasaurus* was found in 1980. The armor consisted of ridged plates on its back. The discovery showed that all titanosaurs may have had armor. This would have been a useful defense.

Titanosaurs had pencil-shaped teeth like *Diplodocus* rather than the spoon-shaped teeth of *Brachiosaurus*. They must have fed like *Diplodocus*, raking the needles from the conifer trees.

Saltasaurus probably pushed its way through the vegetation, its broad back presenting a solid shield of armor to any attacker.

FACTS AND FIGURES

Saltasaurus
(SAWL-tuh-SAW-rus)
Meaning of Name: "Lizard from Salta"—a place in Argentina
Classification: Sauropod
Size, Weight: 40 feet (12 meters) long, 6–8 tons (5–7 tonnes)
Time: Late Cretaceous, 83 to 79 million years ago
Place: Argentina
Food: Plants

Saltasaurus
The tails of the titanosaurs were flexible, and may have been used as props when the animals were rearing up on their hind legs to reach the treetops.

Spiny Long-Necks

When *Dicraeosaurus* was discovered in the 1920s, scientists noted that it had spines inside its neck. In the early 1990s, another spiny diplodocid **sauropod**, *Amargasaurus*, was discovered. These were the first known sauropods with spines.

Dicraeosaurus
***Dicraeosaurus* had a short neck for a diplodocid sauropod. However, the spines on its backbone would have made it look much bigger and fiercer than it really was. This may have helped to scare away enemies.**

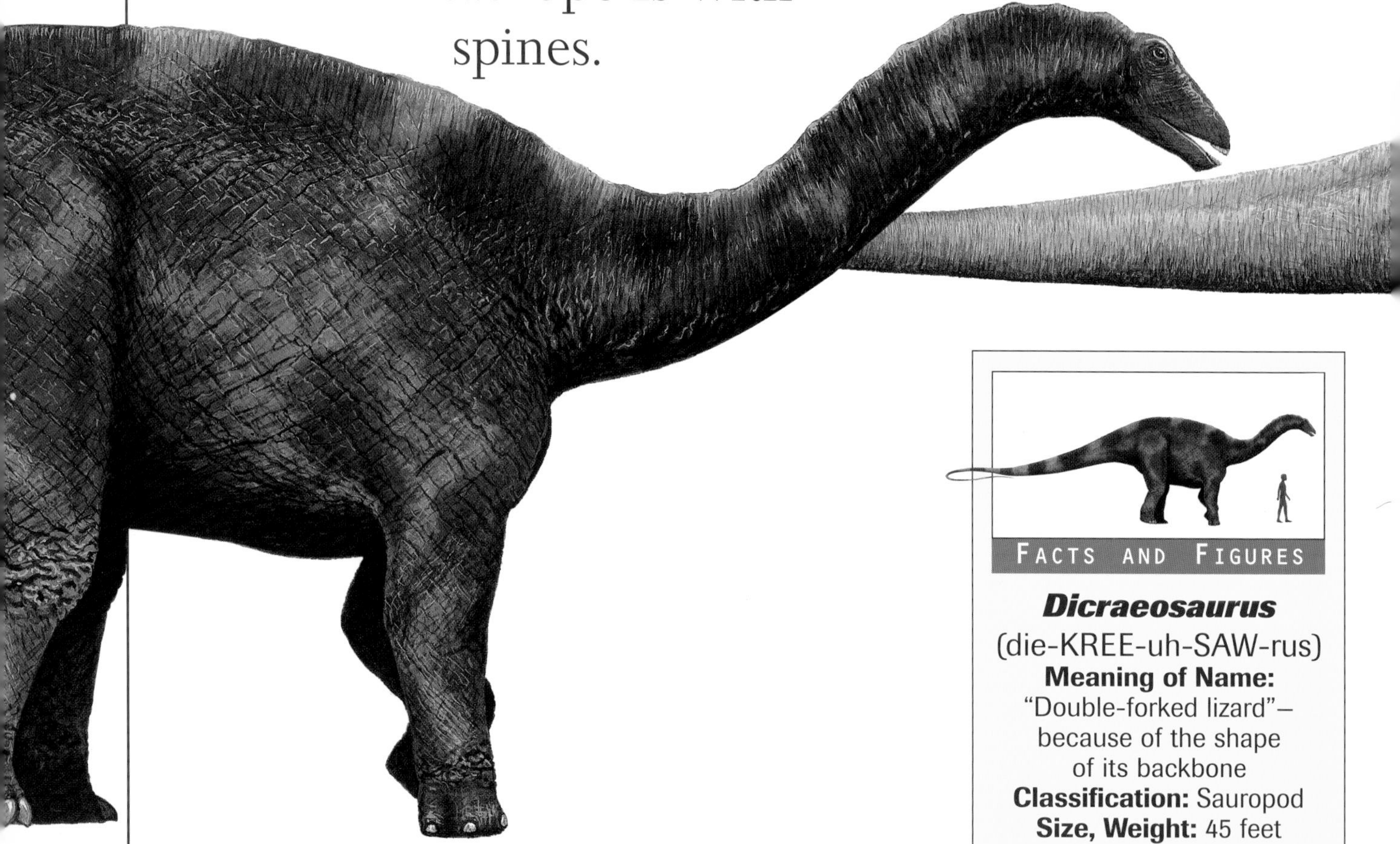

FACTS AND FIGURES

Dicraeosaurus
(die-KREE-uh-SAW-rus)
Meaning of Name: "Double-forked lizard"–because of the shape of its backbone
Classification: Sauropod
Size, Weight: 45 feet (14 meters) long, 10 tons (9 tonnes)
Time: Late Jurassic, 156 to 150 million years ago
Place: East Africa
Food: Plants

In the 1980s, a researcher found a section of tail from a relative of these two *Diplodocus*-like sauropods. A skin impression from the tail showed that it was covered in scales and that a row of horny, cone-shaped points ran down the back.

Amargasaurus
When it was first found, scientists thought that the double row of spines on the neck of *Amargasaurus* supported a pair of fins. They do not think so now because the fins would have made the neck difficult to move.

FACTS AND FIGURES

Amargasaurus
(uh-MAR-guh-SAW-rus)
Meaning of Name: "Lizard from La Amarga"—found in the Amarga canyon in Argentina
Classification: Sauropod
Size, Weight: 33 feet (10 meters) long, 8 tons (7 tonnes)
Time: Early Cretaceous, 131 to 125 million years ago
Place: Argentina
Food: Plants

Last of the Giants

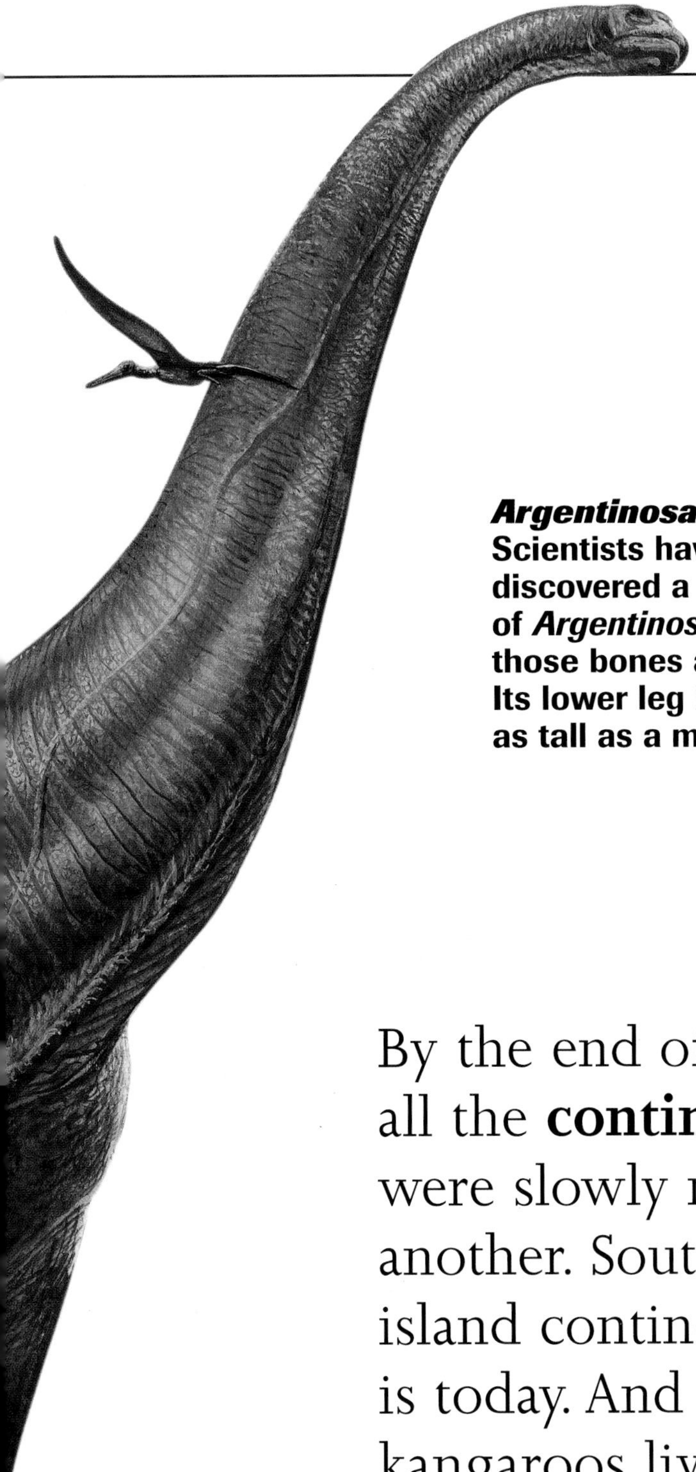

Argentinosaurus
Scientists have only discovered a few bones of *Argentinosaurus*—but those bones are huge. Its lower leg bone is as tall as a man.

FACTS AND FIGURES

Argentinosaurus
(ARE-jen-TEEN-o-SAW-rus)
Meaning of Name: "Lizard from Argentina"
Classification: Sauropod
Size, Weight: 90 feet (29 meters) long, 40 feet (12 meters) high, 100 tons (90 tonnes)
Time: Late Cretaceous, 90 million years ago
Place: Argentina
Food: Leaves

By the end of the **Cretaceous** Period, all the **continents** had split apart and were slowly moving away from one another. South America was one big island continent, just as Australia is today. And just as koala bears and kangaroos live only in Australia, some dinosaurs lived only in South America. These included the meat-eater *Giganotosaurus* and one of the biggest animals ever to have lived on Earth—the plant-eater *Argentinosaurus*.

Vulnerable in Life

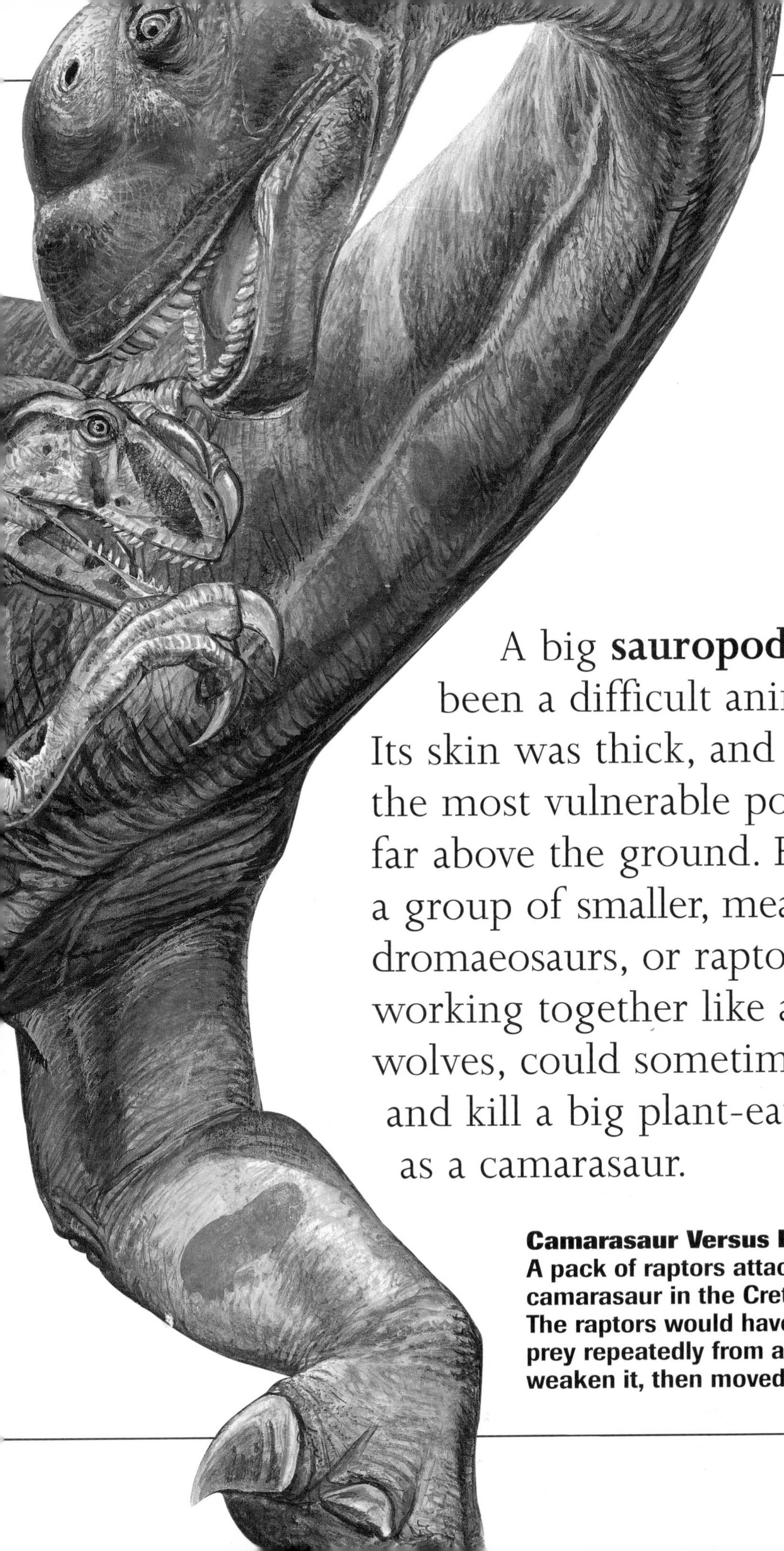

A big **sauropod** must have been a difficult animal to kill. Its skin was thick, and its head—the most vulnerable point—was far above the ground. However, a group of smaller, meat-eating dromaeosaurs, or raptors, working together like a pack of wolves, could sometimes attack and kill a big plant-eater, such as a camarasaur.

Camarasaur Versus Raptor
A pack of raptors attacking a camarasaur in the Cretaceous Period. The raptors would have slashed their prey repeatedly from all sides to weaken it, then moved in for the kill.

Rulers of the Sky

Pterodactylus

Pterodactylus is the best-known pterosaur. Its **fossils** are so well-preserved that scientists can see imprints of its leathery wings.

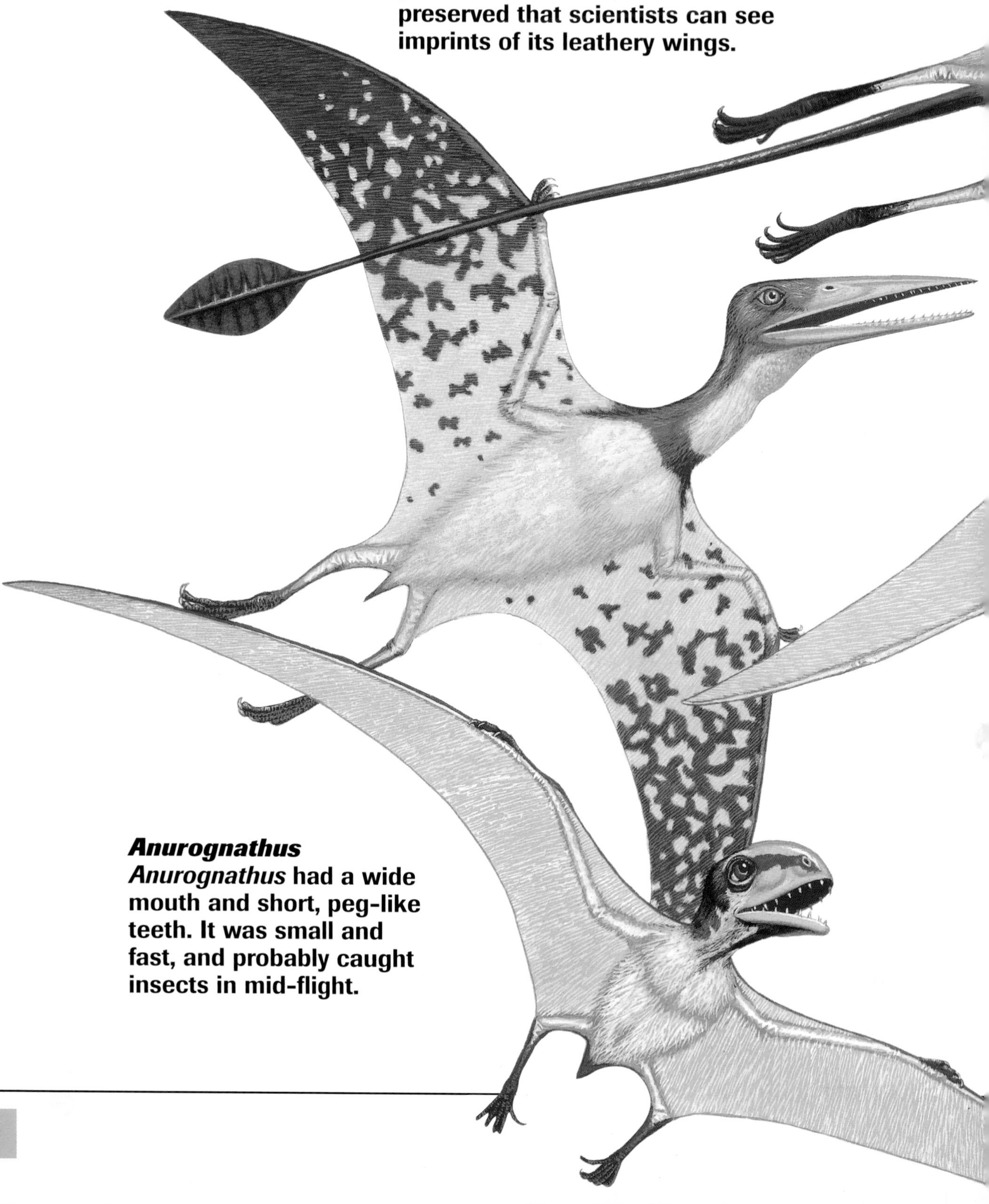

Anurognathus

Anurognathus had a wide mouth and short, peg-like teeth. It was small and fast, and probably caught insects in mid-flight.

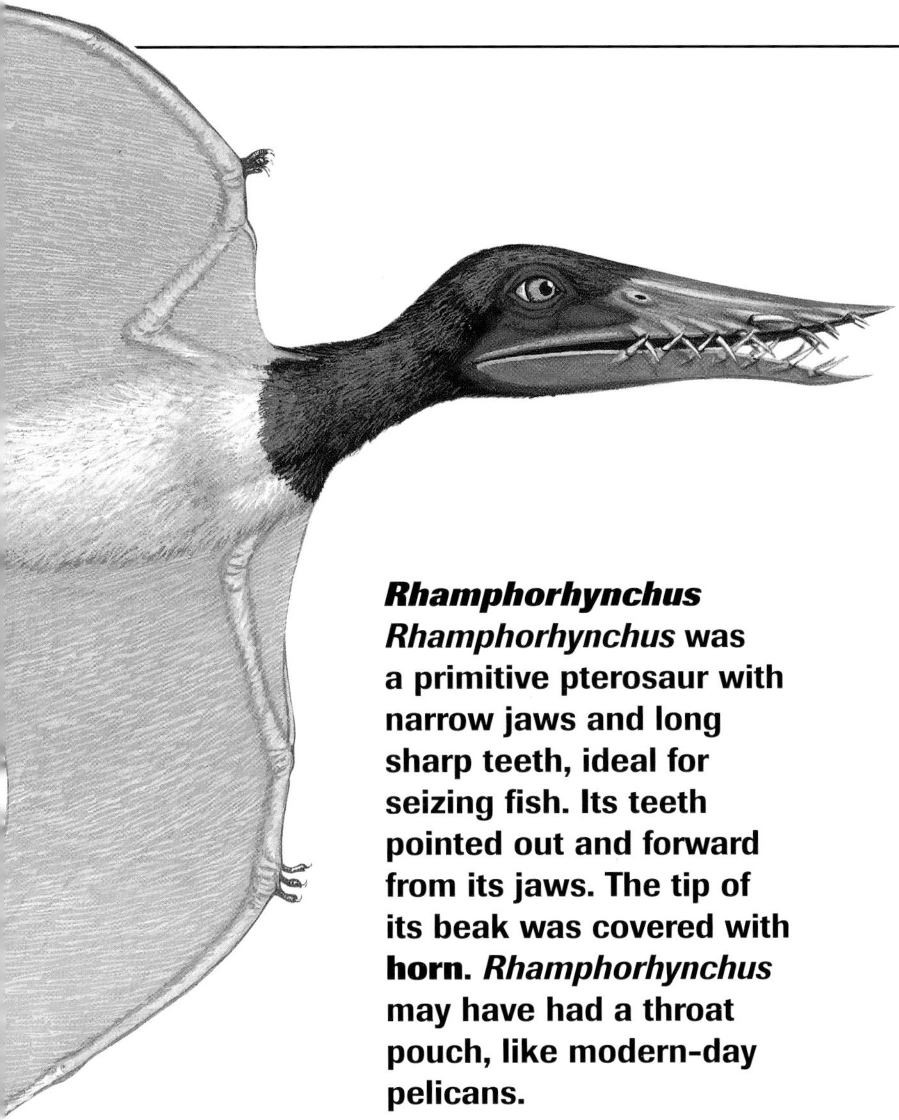

Rhamphorhynchus

Rhamphorhynchus **was a primitive pterosaur with narrow jaws and long sharp teeth, ideal for seizing fish. Its teeth pointed out and forward from its jaws. The tip of its beak was covered with horn.** ***Rhamphorhynchus*** **may have had a throat pouch, like modern-day pelicans.**

Dinosaurs shared their world with many other creatures, including the non-dinosaur flying **reptiles** called **pterosaurs**. Some later pterosaurs were huge. *Quetzalcoatlus* was bigger than a modern hang glider. Others were the size of crows.

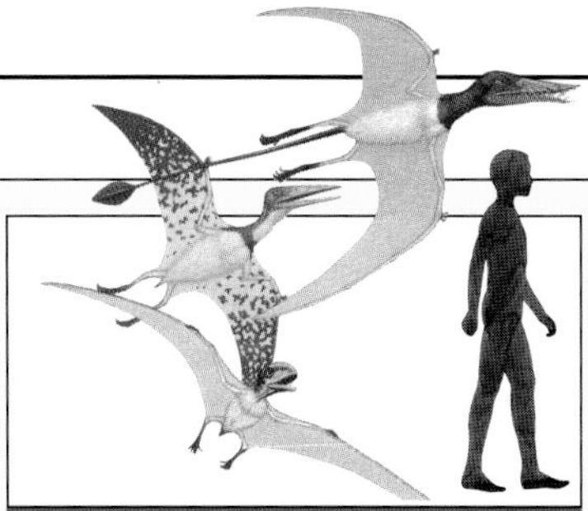

FACTS AND FIGURES

Pterodactylus

(TAIR-o-DACK-till-us)
Meaning of Name: "Wing finger"—after the claws on its wings
Classification: Pterosaur
Size, Weight: 1–8 foot (30–250 centimeter) wingspan, 2–20 pounds (1–9 kilograms)
Time: Late Jurassic, 145 million years ago
Place: Europe and East Africa
Food: Fish

Anurognathus

(an-YOUR-og-NAY-thus)
Meaning of Name: "Jaws without a tail"
Classification: Pterosaur
Size, Weight: 20 inch (51 centimeter) wingspan, 2 pounds (1 kilogram)
Time: Late Jurassic, 145 million years ago
Place: Germany
Food: Insects

Rhamphorhynchus

(RAM-fo-RING-kus)
Meaning of Name: "Beaked snout"
Classification: Pterosaur
Size, Weight: 6 foot (2 meter) wingspan, 15 pounds (7 kilograms)
Time: Late Jurassic, 145 million years ago
Place: Germany and East Africa
Food: Fish

Armored Dinosaurs

The end of the **Cretaceous** Period was the time of the fierce **carnivore** *Tyrannosaurus.* Some plant-eaters developed armor of horns, plates, and spikes, which helped protect them from such meat-eaters.

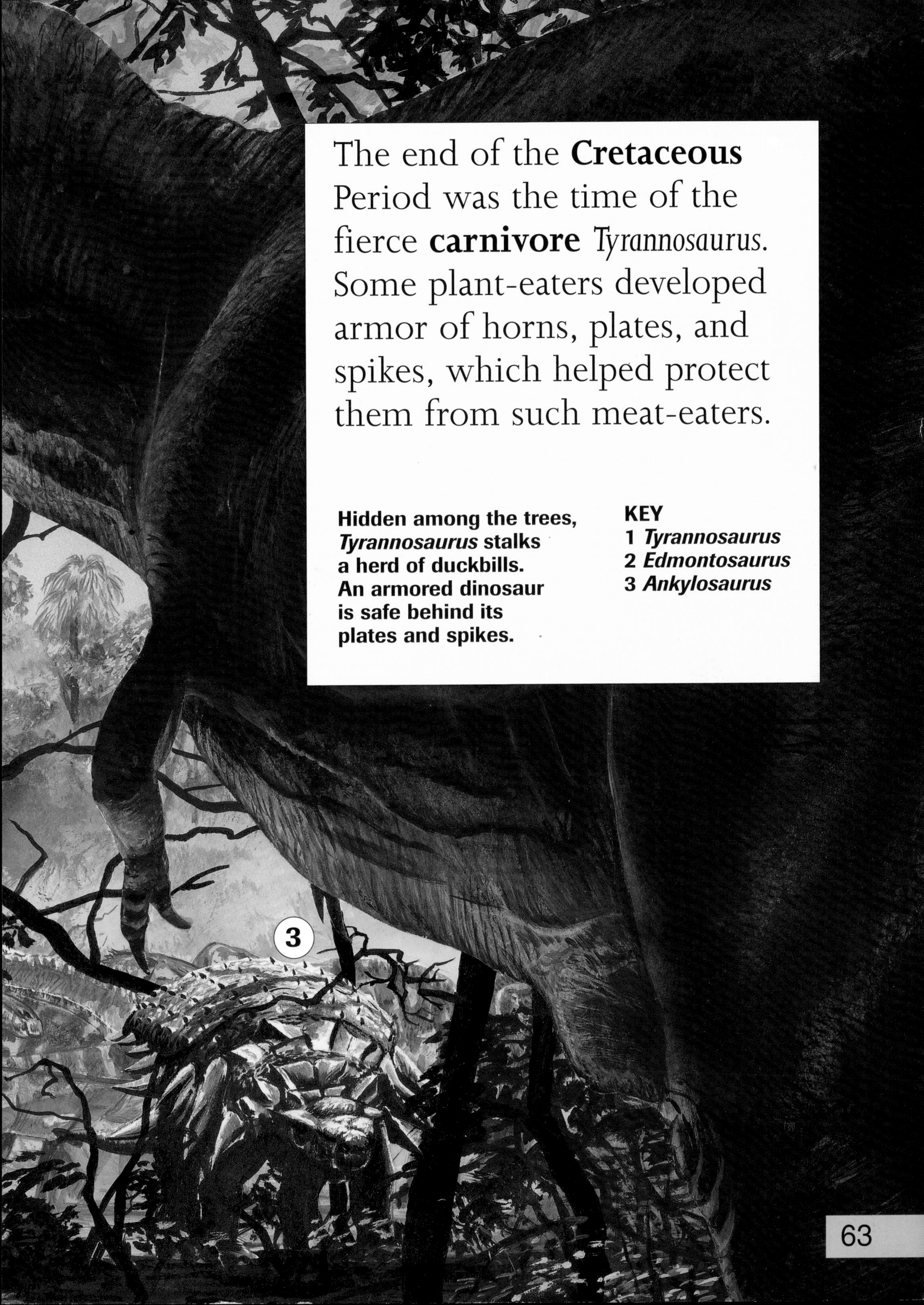

Hidden among the trees, *Tyrannosaurus* stalks a herd of duckbills. An armored dinosaur is safe behind its plates and spikes.

KEY
1 *Tyrannosaurus*
2 *Edmontosaurus*
3 *Ankylosaurus*

Many Defenses

By the end of the **Cretaceous** Period, plant-eaters had **evolved** different ways of defending themselves from meat-eaters. Some of them got tough by developing horns, armor, and clubs.

Look at *Triceratops* with its head full of horns and at *Euoplocephalus* with its armor-covered back. These were among the biggest and last of the armor-bearers. There were all sorts of other armored dinosaurs, and they existed throughout the Age of Dinosaurs.

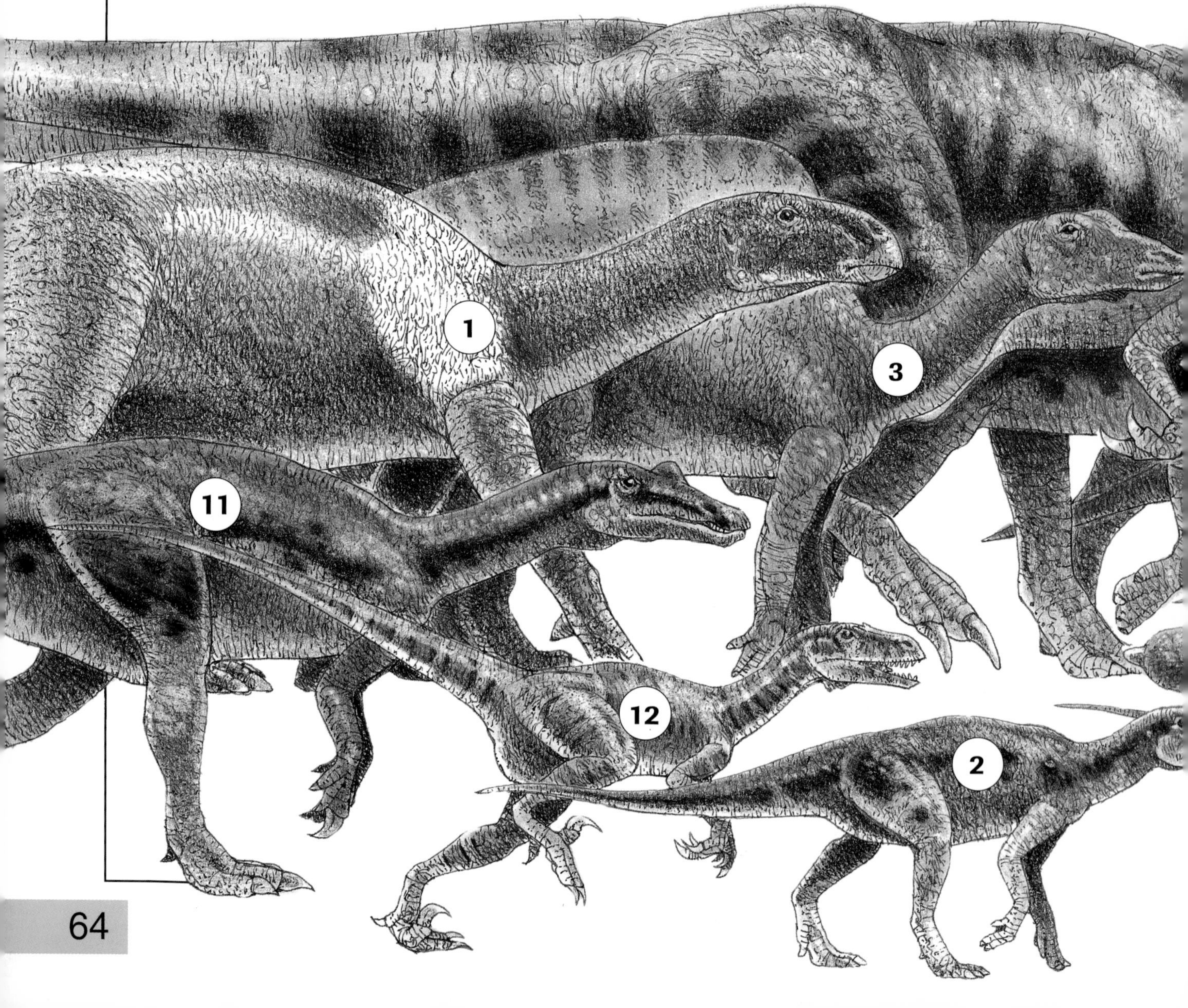

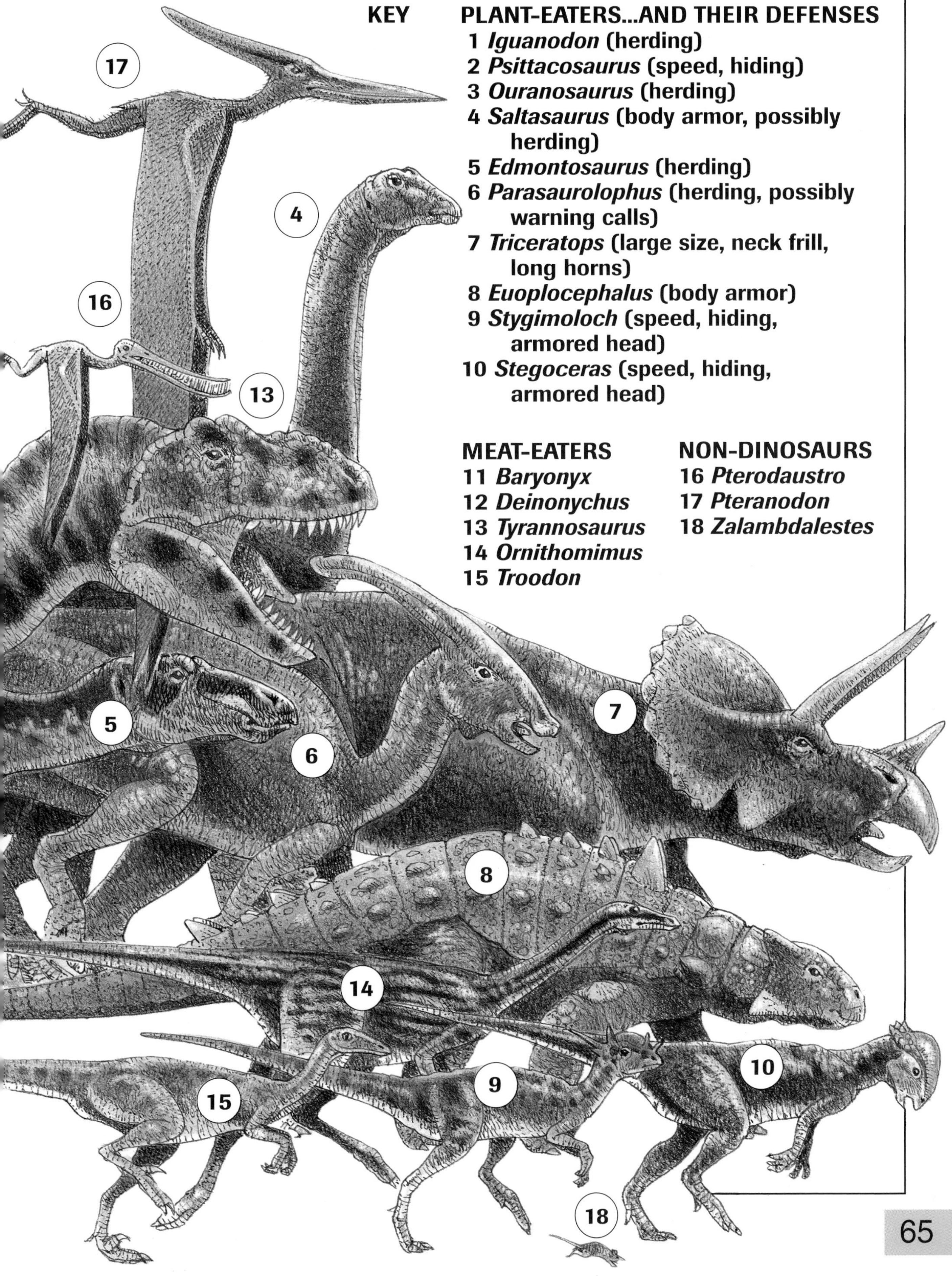

KEY

PLANT-EATERS...AND THEIR DEFENSES

1 *Iguanodon* (herding)
2 *Psittacosaurus* (speed, hiding)
3 *Ouranosaurus* (herding)
4 *Saltasaurus* (body armor, possibly herding)
5 *Edmontosaurus* (herding)
6 *Parasaurolophus* (herding, possibly warning calls)
7 *Triceratops* (large size, neck frill, long horns)
8 *Euoplocephalus* (body armor)
9 *Stygimoloch* (speed, hiding, armored head)
10 *Stegoceras* (speed, hiding, armored head)

MEAT-EATERS

11 *Baryonyx*
12 *Deinonychus*
13 *Tyrannosaurus*
14 *Ornithomimus*
15 *Troodon*

NON-DINOSAURS

16 *Pterodaustro*
17 *Pteranodon*
18 *Zalambdalestes*

Early Armor

By the Late **Triassic** and Early **Jurassic** periods, there were many meat-eating dinosaurs around. There were also other meat-eaters, such as crocodiles.

Scelidosaurus
Scelidosaurus **was the size of a small cow. It had rows of bony knobs running from its skull to the tip of its tail.**

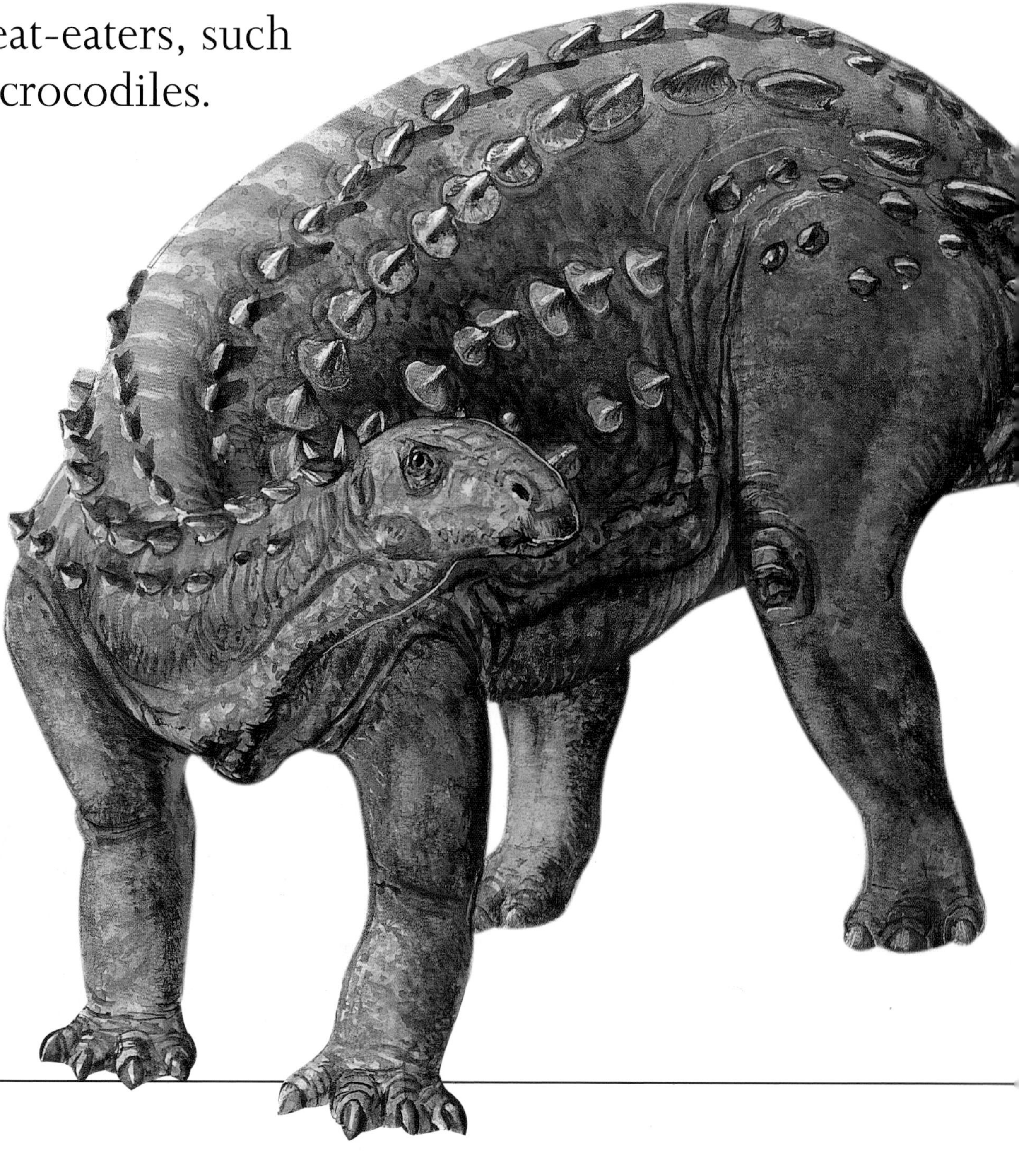

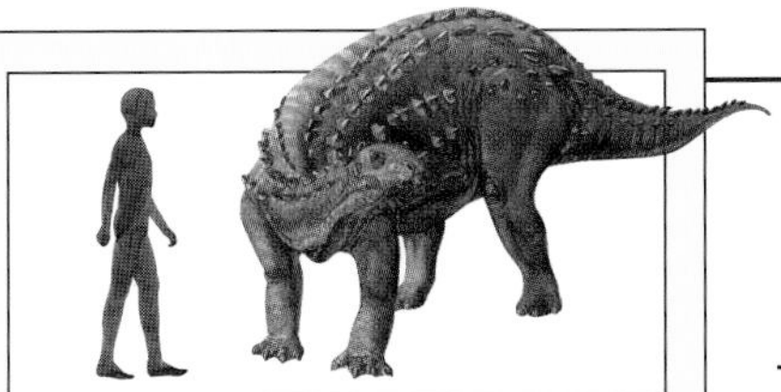

FACTS AND FIGURES

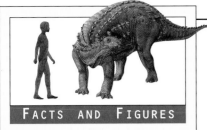

Scelidosaurus
(skel-EYE-doe-SAW-rus)
Meaning of Name: "Leg lizard"—early scientists thought its legs were different from those of any other reptile
Classification: Scelidosaur, may be ancestor to the stegosaurs and ankylosaurs
Size, Weight: 13 feet (4 meters) long, 500 pounds (227 kilograms)
Time: Early Jurassic, 208 to 200 million years ago
Place: England
Food: Plants

At this time, some of the plant-eaters began to develop armor to defend themselves against these hungry **predators**. The first armor was on the back and consisted of small bony knobs, or shields. If attacked, the armored dinosaur would crouch on the ground so its attacker would get a mouthful of hard, tough bone.

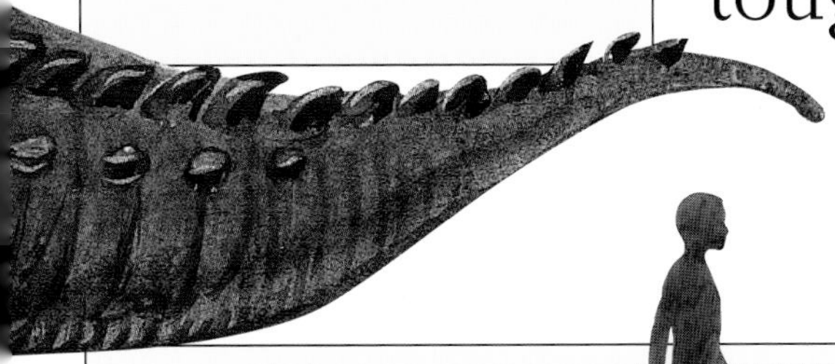

FACTS AND FIGURES

Scutellosaurus
(skoo-TELL-o-SAW-rus)
Meaning of Name: "Lizard with little shields"
Classification: Uncertain, may be related to both stegosaurs and ankylosaurs
Size, Weight: 4 feet (120 centimeters) long, 20 pounds (9 kilograms)
Time: Early Jurassic, 208 to 200 million years ago
Place: Arizona
Food: Plants

Scutellosaurus
Scutellosaurus **must have looked like a knobby lizard with a very long tail. Its back was covered with more than 300 bony studs and spikes.**

Plate-Bearers

The **stegosaurs** were plate-carrying dinosaurs. Their armor consisted of a double row of pointed plates running along the length of their backs. Most stegosaurs also had a double row of spikes on the end of their tails, which they used as weapons. If in danger, they could swing their tails at their attackers with great force. Some stegosaurs, such as *Kentrosaurus*, also had long spikes sticking out from their shoulders. These helped to protect them if they were attacked from the front or the sides.

Kentrosaurus
Kentrosaurus **was the size of a large cow. It had narrow, pointed spikes on its neck and back, and long spikes on its tail.**

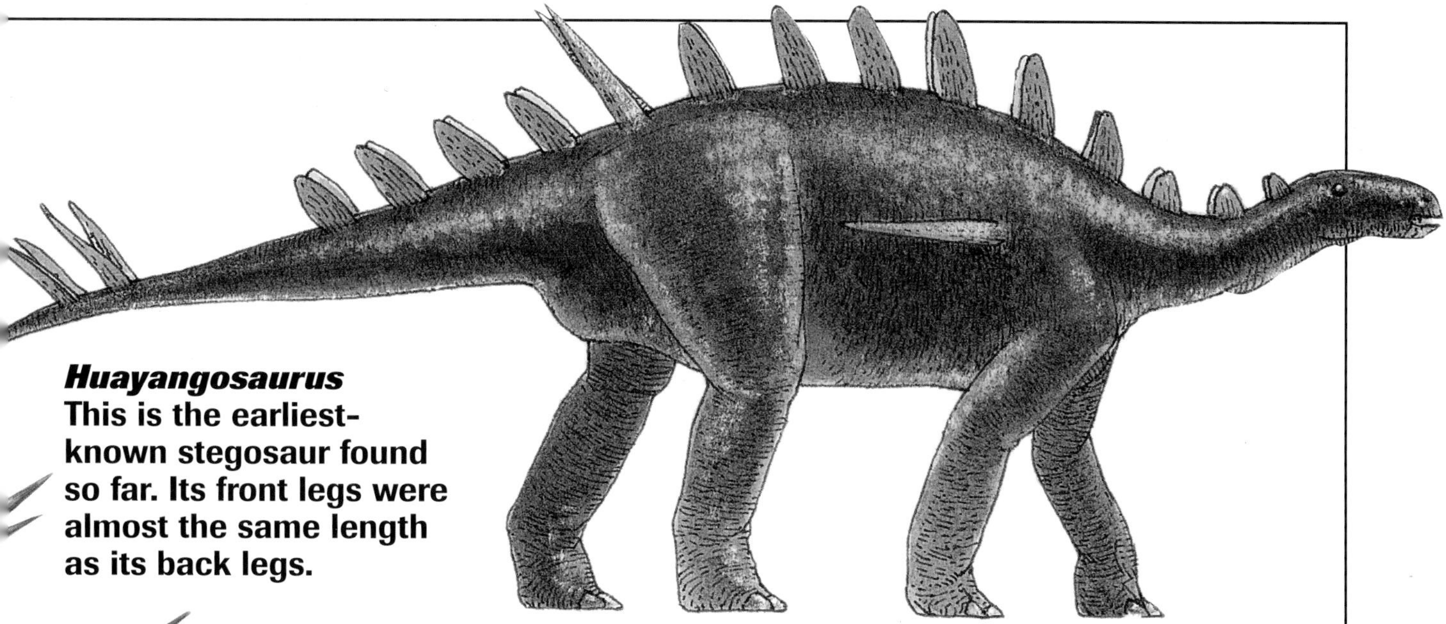

Huayangosaurus
This is the earliest-known stegosaur found so far. Its front legs were almost the same length as its back legs.

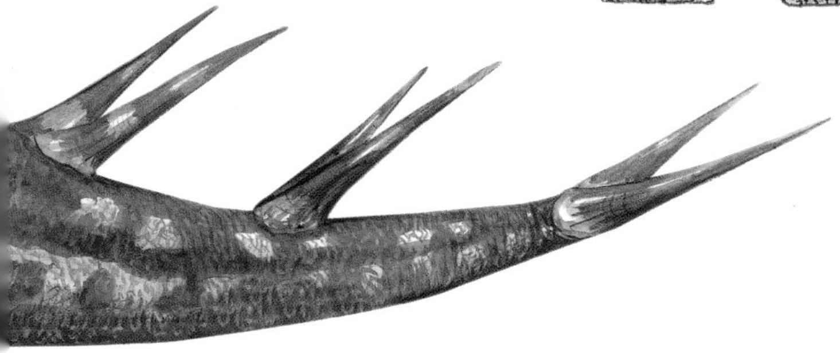

FACTS AND FIGURES

Kentrosaurus
(KEN-tro-SAW-rus)
Meaning of Name: "Spiked lizard"
Classification: Stegosaur, the main group of stegosaurs
Size, Weight: 16 feet (5 meters) long, up to 4,000 pounds (1,800 kilograms)
Time: Late Jurassic, 155 to 150 million years ago
Place: Tanzania, East Africa
Food: Plants

Food for All
The plated dinosaurs were usually smaller than the long-necked plant-eating dinosaurs. They probably ate the lower branches of tall ginkgo trees or plants that grew closer to the ground, such as tough cycads.

FACTS AND FIGURES

Huayangosaurus
(hwi-YANG-o-SAW-rus)
Meaning of Name: "Lizard from Huayang" (now Sichuan)—a province in China
Classification: Huayangosaur, one of the groups of stegosaurs, the plated dinosaurs
Size, Weight: 13 feet (4 meters) long, up to 1 ton (almost 1 tonne)
Time: Middle Jurassic, 166–157 million years ago
Place: China
Food: Plants

Big Plate-Carrier

Stegosaurus is probably the best-known **stegosaur**. It had a spiked tail and rows of wide triangular plates running down its back. Scientists are still not sure what the plates were used for.

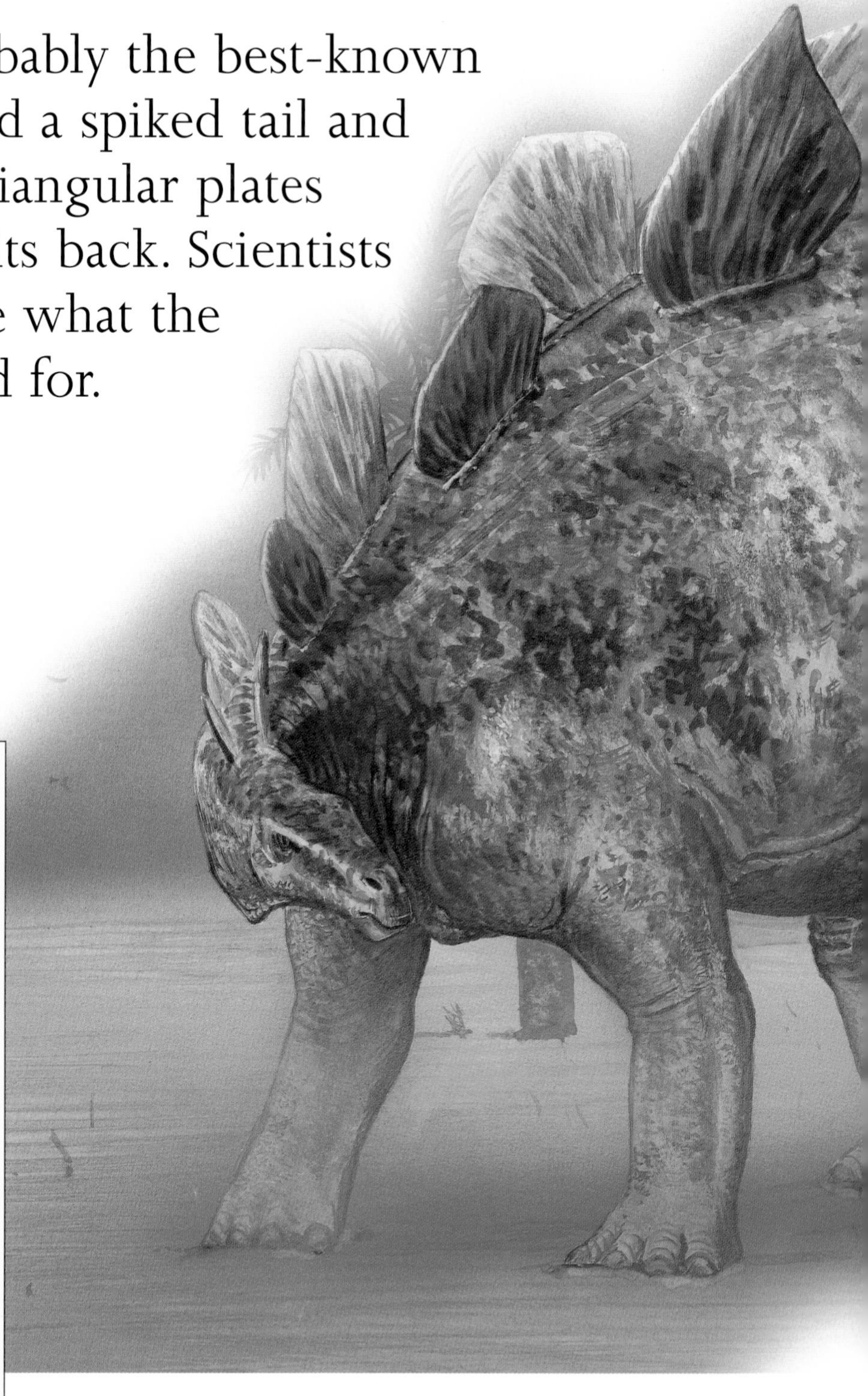

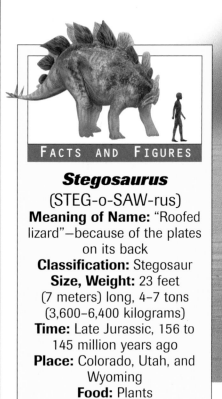

FACTS AND FIGURES

Stegosaurus
(STEG-o-SAW-rus)
Meaning of Name: "Roofed lizard"—because of the plates on its back
Classification: Stegosaur
Size, Weight: 23 feet (7 meters) long, 4–7 tons (3,600–6,400 kilograms)
Time: Late Jurassic, 156 to 145 million years ago
Place: Colorado, Utah, and Wyoming
Food: Plants

Spiked Tails

If attacked, dinosaurs such as *Stegosaurus* or *Huayangosaurus* would turn their backs toward their predators and lash out with their long, spiked tails. Their tails were not powerful enough to kill a big predator, but they might have forced an enemy to look for an easier meal elsewhere.

Stegosaurus
Stegosaurus **had a very small head for the size of its body. Like other armored dinosaurs, it had a beak and might have had cheek pouches, to help it gather food.**

Stegosaurus's plates may have been used as armor. If so, they would have been covered with **horn**. Perhaps the plates were used to keep the dinosaur cool, rather like the cooling fins of a motorcycle engine. If so, they would have been covered in skin.

Spikes and Armor

The **stegosaurs** were the main armored dinosaurs of the **Jurassic** Period, but they died out during the **Cretaceous** Period. Their place was taken by the **ankylosaurs**. There were two groups of ankylosaurs—nodosaurids, which had spikes on their backs and sides, and ankylosaurids, which had clubs on their tails.

Minmi
Often, dinosaurs have long jaw-cracking names. *Minmi* is the shortest dinosaur name on record so far. Like other nodosaurids, *Minmi* did not have a club on its tail.

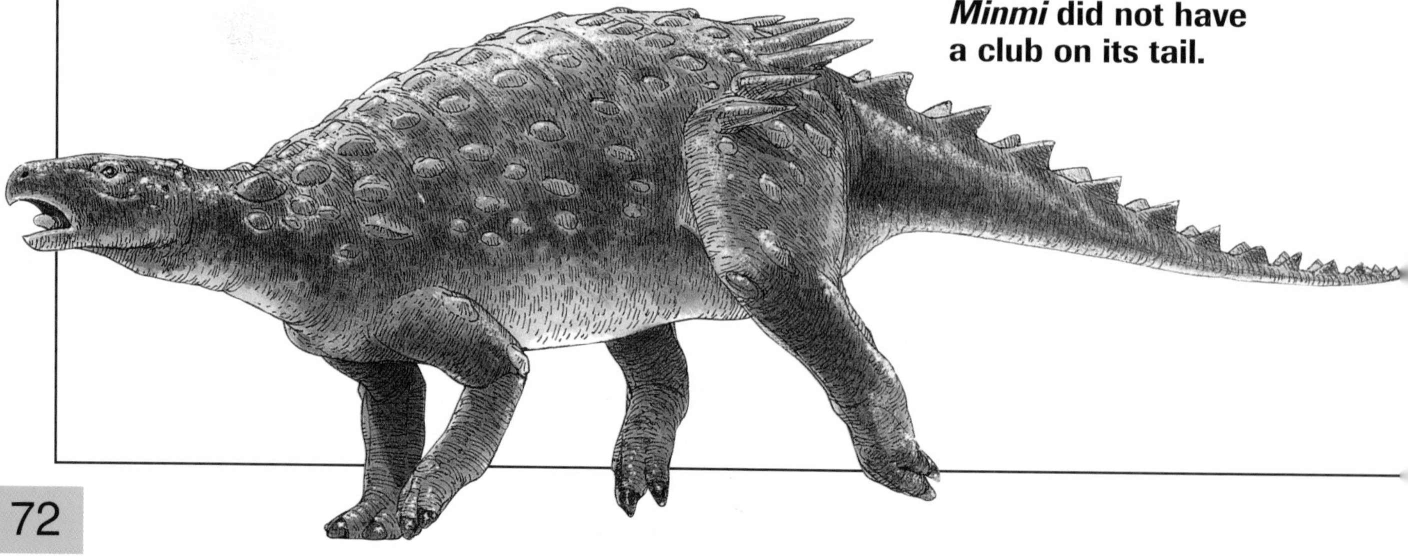

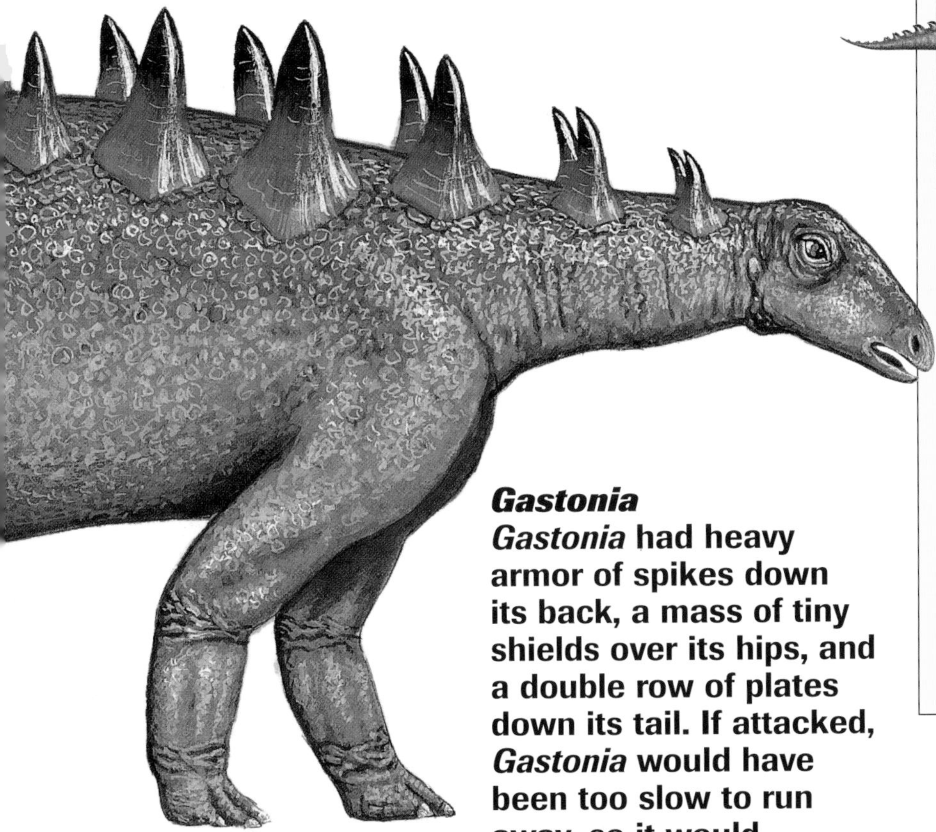

FACTS AND FIGURES

Gastonia

(gas-TOE-nee-uh)

Meaning of Name: "Gaston's animal"—after Robert Gaston, who discovered it

Classification: Nodosaur

Size, Weight: 20 feet (6 meters) long, 2 tons (1,800 kilograms)

Time: Early Cretaceous, 132–125 million years ago

Place: Utah

Food: Plants

Gastonia

Gastonia had heavy armor of spikes down its back, a mass of tiny shields over its hips, and a double row of plates down its tail. If attacked, _Gastonia_ would have been too slow to run away, so it would have crouched to protect its delicate underbelly.

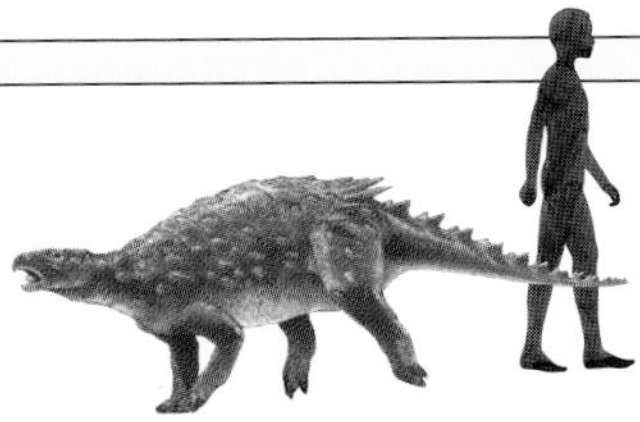

FACTS AND FIGURES

Minmi

(MIN-mee)

Meaning of Name: "Found at Minmi Crossing"—a place in Australia

Classification: Nodosaur, a group of ankylosaurs without tail clubs

Size, Weight: 9 feet (3 meters) long, 500 pounds (227 kilograms)

Time: Early Cretaceous, 119 to 113 million years ago

Place: Australia

Food: Plants

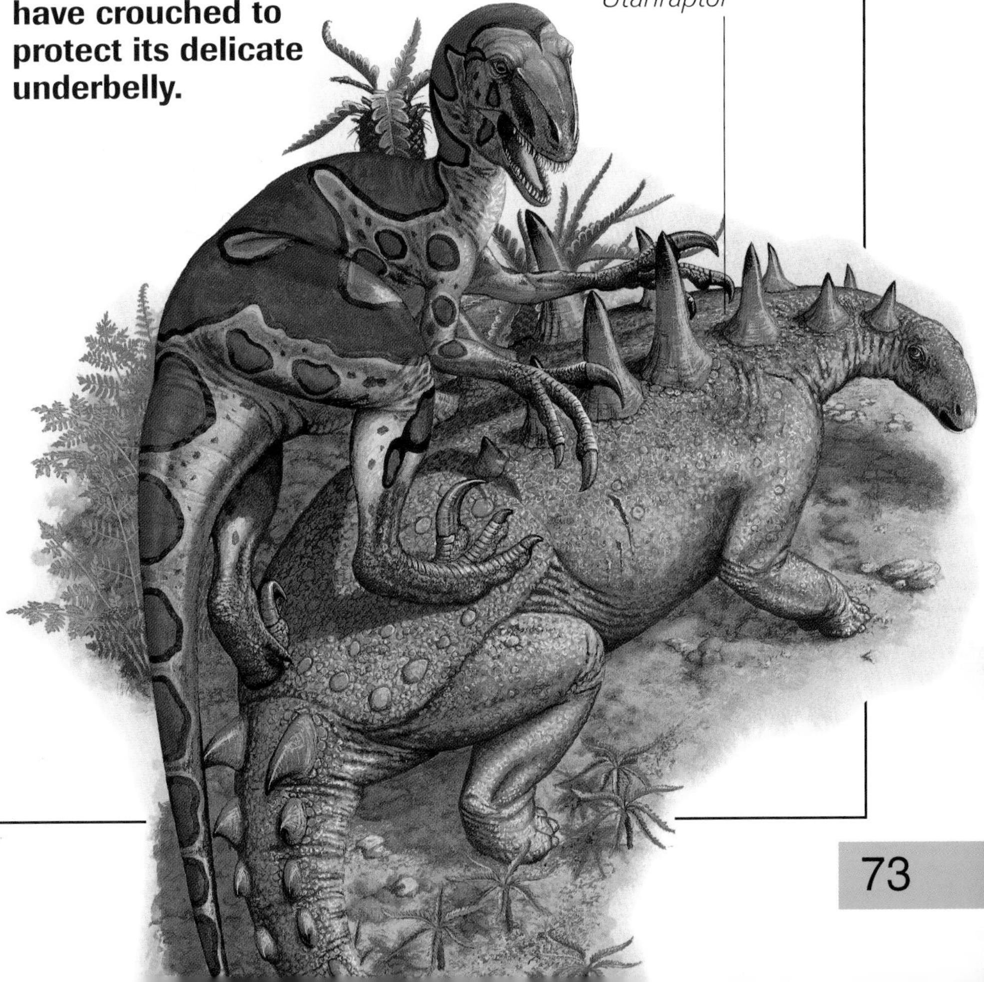

Gastonia defending itself against *Utahraptor*

Side Spikes

The bigger nodosaurs had huge spikes sticking out of their armored shoulders. These would have scared away many meat-eaters. If a nodosaur were actually attacked, then it would have used its spikes for fighting.

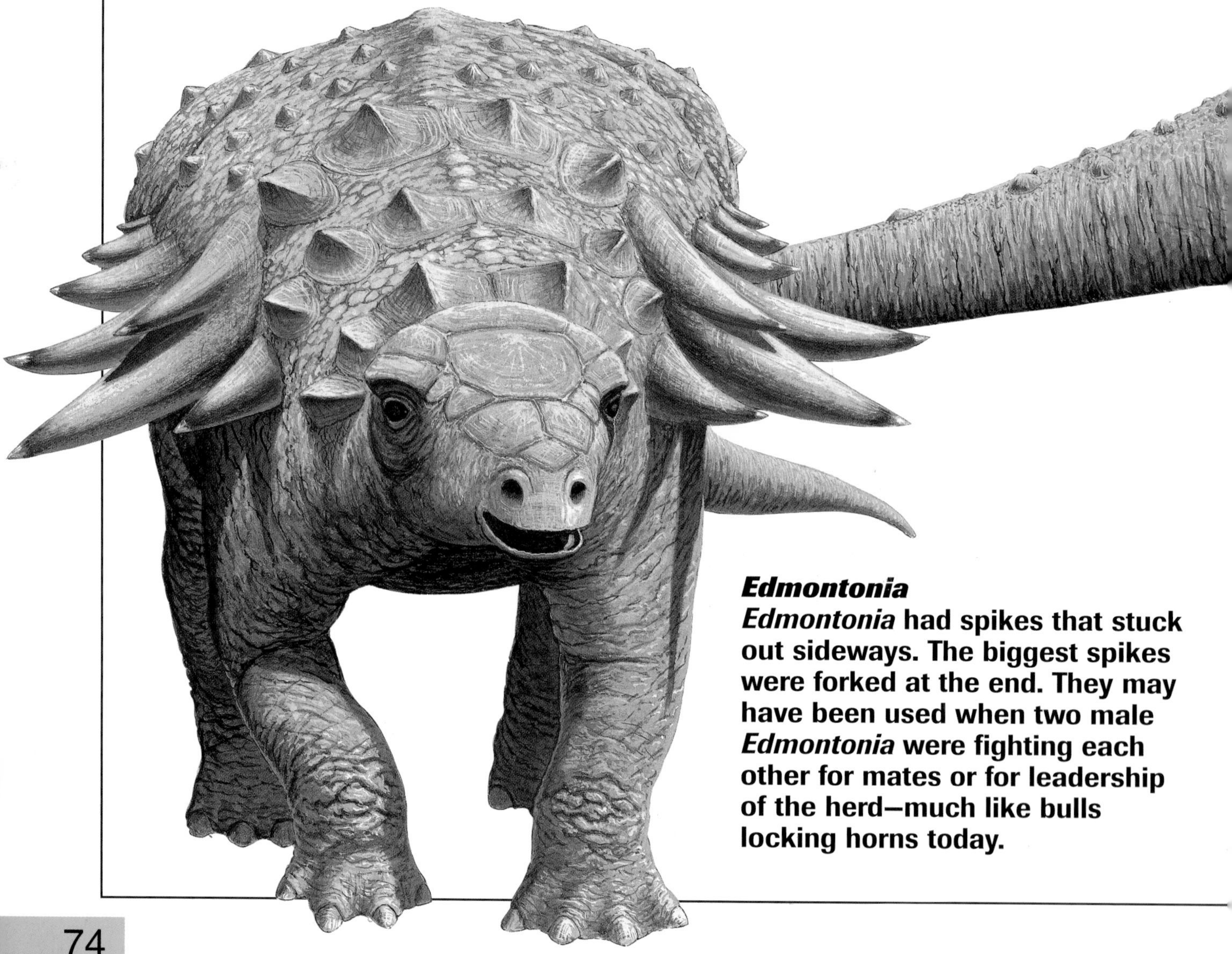

Edmontonia
Edmontonia had spikes that stuck out sideways. The biggest spikes were forked at the end. They may have been used when two male *Edmontonia* were fighting each other for mates or for leadership of the herd—much like bulls locking horns today.

FACTS AND FIGURES

Edmontonia

(ED-mawn-TOE-nee-uh)

Meaning of Name: "From Edmonton"—the capital of Alberta, Canada, where it is found
Classification: Nodosaur
Size, Weight: 23 feet (7 meters) long, 3 tons (2,700 kilograms)
Time: Late Cretaceous, 76 to 68 million years ago
Place: Canada
Food: Plants

FACTS AND FIGURES

Sauropelta

(SAW-ro-PEL-tuh)

Meaning of Name: "Shield lizard"
Classification: Nodosaur
Size, Weight: 20 feet (6 meters) long, 3 tons (2,700 kilograms)
Time: Early Cretaceous, 116 to 97 million years ago
Place: Montana and Wyoming
Food: Plants

Sauropelta

***Sauropelta* had shoulder spikes that stuck upward, making the dinosaur look bigger and fiercer than it really was.**

The rest of the armor consisted of broad oval plates on the neck and hollow triangular plates on the back and tail.

***Sauropelta* was the earliest known of the nodosaurs. It was a common animal living in the Early Cretaceous.**

Tail-Clubber

Quick on Its Feet
Even though it had very heavy armor, *Ankylosaurus* was agile and would have been able to react quickly if it were attacked by a large meat-eating dinosaur, such as *Albertosaurus*.

Ankylosaurs had a powerful weapon. Each had a massive lump of bone at the end of its tail. The tail bones were shaped to link together so that an ankylosaur held its tail stiff and straight, like the shaft, or handle, of a club.

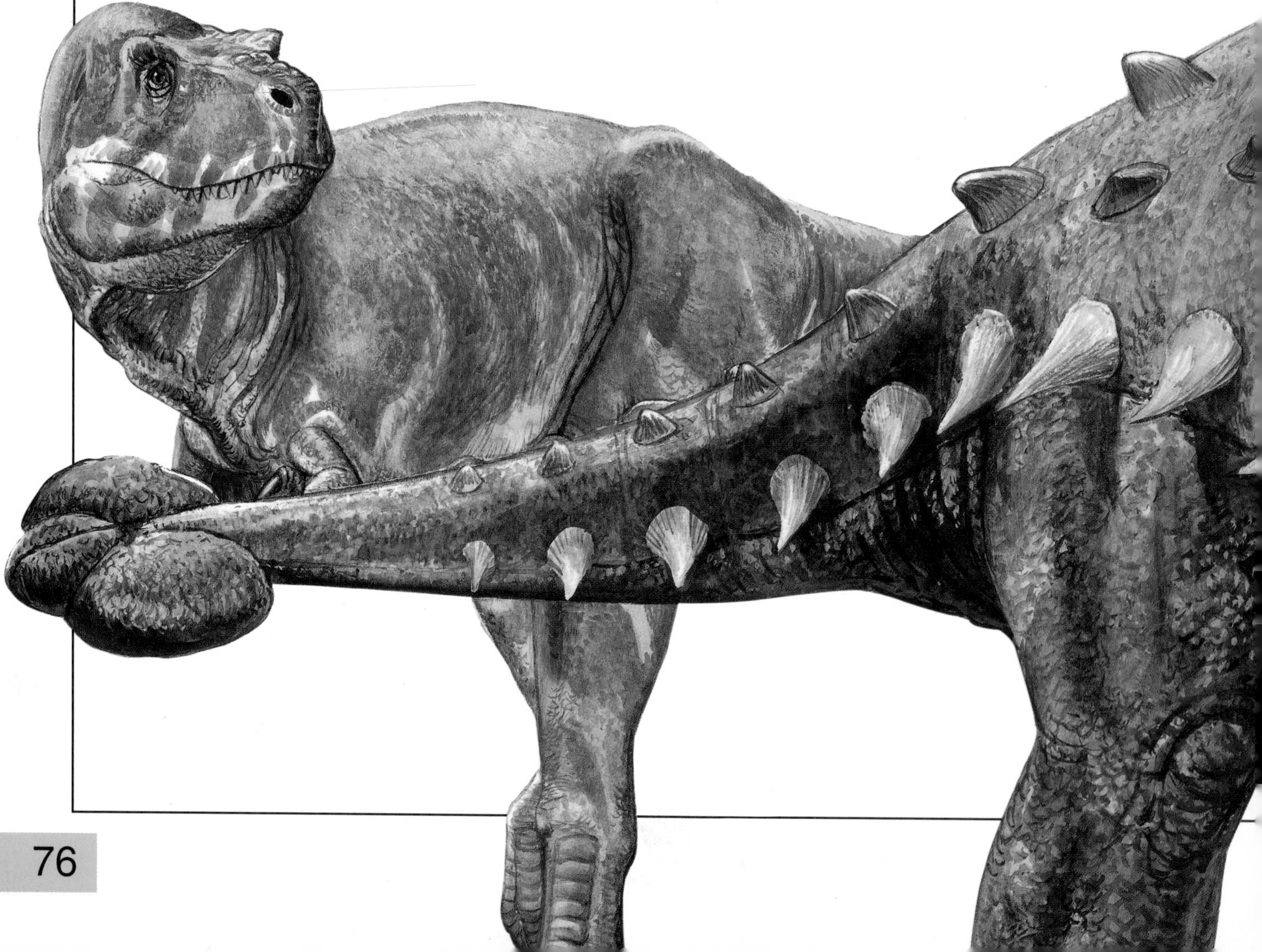

FACTS AND FIGURES

Ankylosaurus
(ang-KY-lo-SAW-rus)
Meaning of Name: "Fused lizard"—the plates on its back were fused, or fixed, together to form armor
Classification: Ankylosaur
Size, Weight: 25 feet (8 meters) long, 3 tons (2,700 kilograms)
Time: Late Cretaceous, 68 to 65 million years ago
Place: Alberta, Wyoming, Montana
Food: Plants

The ankylosaurs had strong hip muscles. They could swing their tails to the side with such force that their tail clubs could smash the legs of an attacking meat-eater. The ankylosaurs were reptilian tanks!

Ankylosaurus
***Ankylosaurus*, the most heavily armored dinosaur, was the biggest and the last of the ankylosaurs. Its skull was a box of armored bone. Even its eyelids were armored, slamming shut when danger approached.**

Colorful Clubs

We do not know what colors dinosaurs were. Perhaps the meat-eaters could see in color. In that case, it would have been useful if a plant-eater were **camouflaged** and could blend into the **vegetation**. Perhaps plant-eaters were a lighter color underneath so that the shadows on the undersides of their bodies would not show up so well.

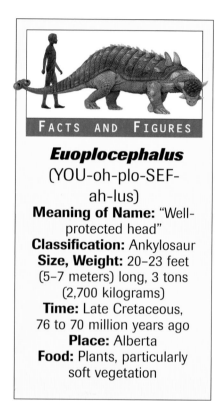

FACTS AND FIGURES

Euoplocephalus
(YOU-oh-plo-SEF-ah-lus)
Meaning of Name: "Well-protected head"
Classification: Ankylosaur
Size, Weight: 20–23 feet (5–7 meters) long, 3 tons (2,700 kilograms)
Time: Late Cretaceous, 76 to 70 million years ago
Place: Alberta
Food: Plants, particularly soft vegetation

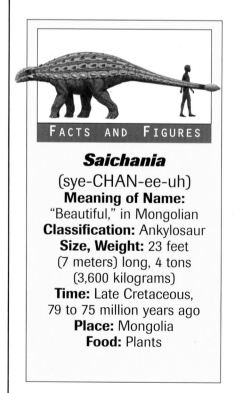

FACTS AND FIGURES

Saichania
(sye-CHAN-ee-uh)
Meaning of Name: "Beautiful," in Mongolian
Classification: Ankylosaur
Size, Weight: 23 feet (7 meters) long, 4 tons (3,600 kilograms)
Time: Late Cretaceous, 79 to 75 million years ago
Place: Mongolia
Food: Plants

Some scientists think that the ankylosaurs had bright colors on their tail clubs. If these bright colors were in the shape of a pair of eyes, then an attacking meat-eater might attack the club instead of the head—and get a bony mouthful!

Euoplocephalus
Euoplocephalus **is the best-known of the ankylosaurs. Its heavy armor** ***fossilized*** **easily, and a number of skeletons have been found.**

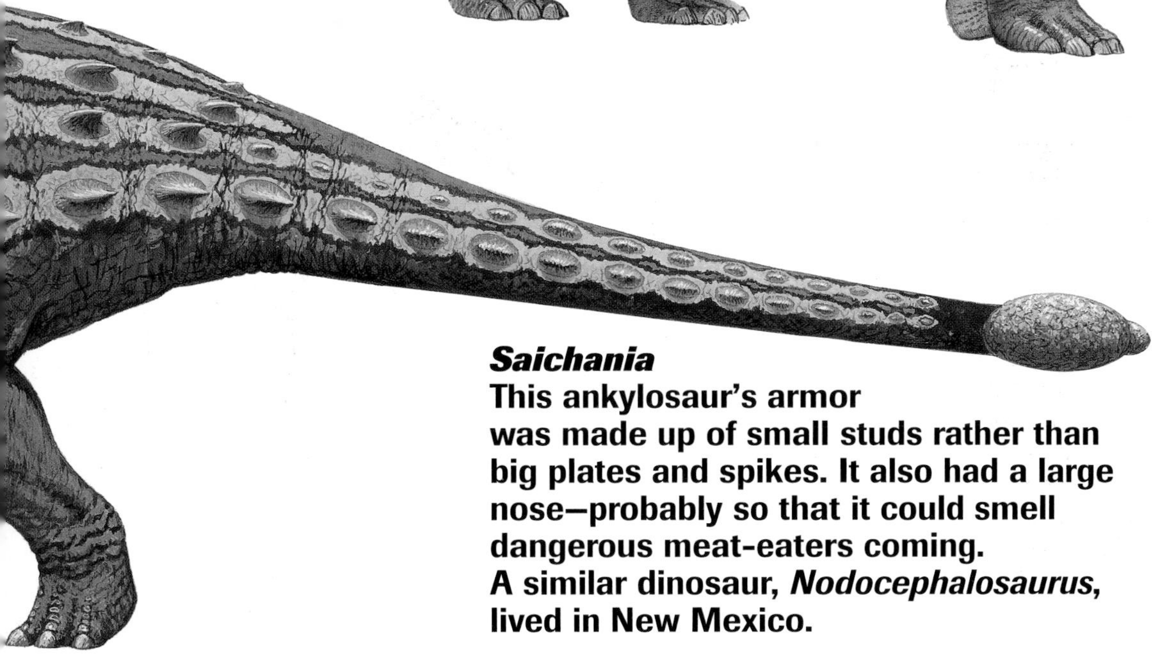

Saichania
This ankylosaur's armor was made up of small studs rather than big plates and spikes. It also had a large nose—probably so that it could smell dangerous meat-eaters coming. A similar dinosaur, ***Nodocephalosaurus*****, lived in New Mexico.**

Beginnings of Horns

The **ceratopsians** were horned dinosaurs. Early ceratopsians, however, were very small and did not have big neck frills or **horns** like the ceratopsians living at the end of the Age of Dinosaurs. Early ceratopsians could run about on their hind legs or on all fours.

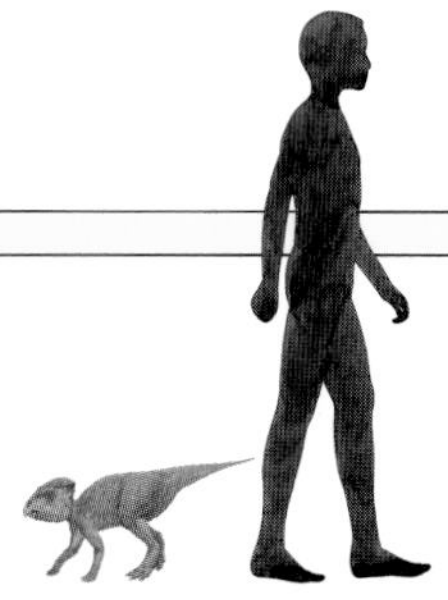

FACTS AND FIGURES

Archaeoceratops
(ARE-kee-o-SAIR-uh-tops)
Meaning of Name: "Ancient horned face"
Classification: Protoceratopsid, a group of small ceratopsians
Size, Weight: 2 feet (70 centimeters) long, 2 pounds (1 kilogram)
Time: Late Cretaceous, 97 to 90 million years ago
Place: China
Food: Plants

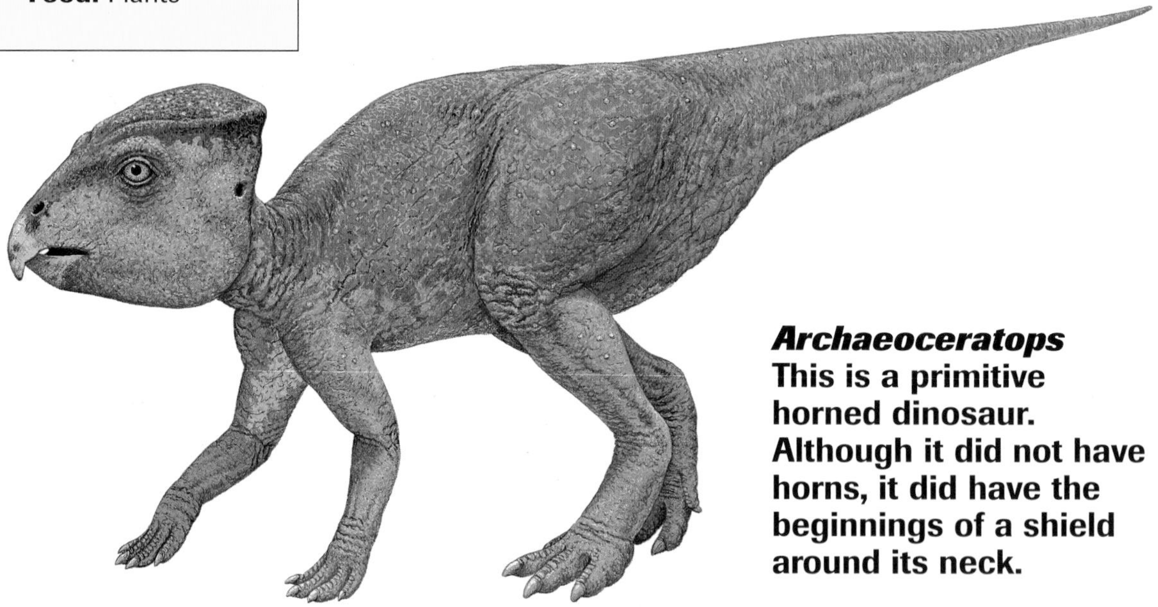

Archaeoceratops
This is a primitive horned dinosaur. Although it did not have horns, it did have the beginnings of a shield around its neck.

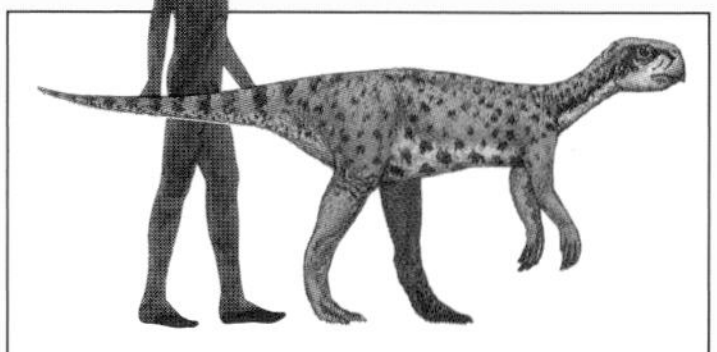

FACTS AND FIGURES

Psittacosaurus
(si-TACK-o-SAW-rus)
Meaning of Name: "Parrot lizard"–it had a square head and large beak, like those of a parrot
Classification: Psittacosaur, the most primitive of the ceratopsians, or horned dinosaurs
Size, Weight: 6 feet (2 meters) long, 50 pounds (23 kilograms)
Time: Early Cretaceous, 119 to 97 million years ago
Place: Mongolia, China, and Thailand
Food: Plants, perhaps tough stems and fruits

At first, neck frills were simple ridges that helped to hold strong jaw muscles. These muscles gave the animals a powerful bite so they could eat tough seeds and nuts. The ridges slowly **evolved** into huge armored frills.

Psittacosaurus
Psittacosaurus **lived in dry, desert-like areas, where it walked on two legs instead of four. Its large beak was suited for eating tough plants, and the ridge on the back of its skull gave its head a square shape.**

A Single Horn

The ceratopsids were the big horned dinosaurs. They all looked similar except for the decorations on their heads. Some had one **horn**. Some had three. Others had several horns growing from the top of their armored neck frills.

Centrosaurus
Centrosaurus **had one large horn on its nose. The frill on its head had jagged edges and two hook-like horns.**

End of a Herd
The remains of more than 300 centrosaurs were found in Alberta, Canada. The herd had probably drowned as it crossed a river.

FACTS AND FIGURES

Centrosaurus
(SEN-tro-SAW-rus)
Meaning of Name: "Sharp-pointed lizard"
Classification: Ceratopsid, the group of big ceratopsians
Size, Weight: 17 feet (550 centimeters) long, 1–2 tons (900–1,800 kilograms)
Time: Late Cretaceous, 76 to 72 million years ago
Place: Alberta
Food: Plants

Many kinds of ceratopsids lived together in the same place. They could recognize one another by the horns on their heads, just as different kinds of antelope living around the same water hole do today.

Big Frills

The frills of the **ceratopsians** were probably used to scare away enemies and to fight them off. The frills may have been brightly colored, with bold patterns and markings. This would have made the dinosaurs look bigger and fiercer than they really were.

Styracosaurus
If attacked, a herd of *Styracosaurus* may have grouped together so that the huge horns of the adults pointed outward, forming a spiky wall.

Styracosaurus
Styracosaurus had a long single horn on its nose and spiky horns around the edge of its neck frill. Its skin may have had bold markings, such as stripes and swirls.

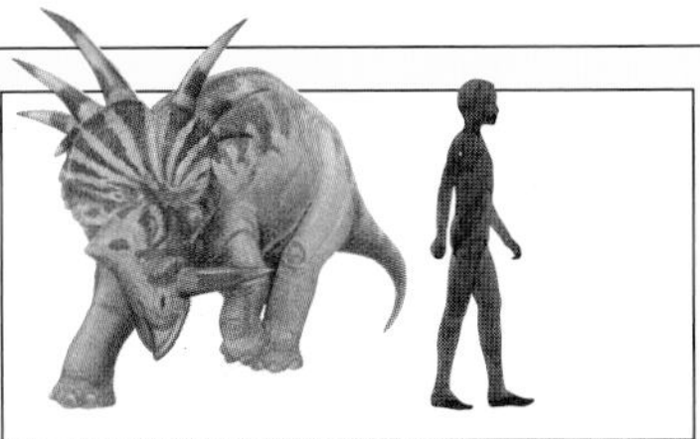

FACTS AND FIGURES

Styracosaurus

(sty-RACK-o-SAW-rus)

Meaning of Name: "Spike lizard"–after a weapon bristling with spikes

Classification: Ceratopsid

Size, Weight: 18 feet (560 centimeters) long, 1–2 tons (900–1,800 kilograms)

Time: Late Cretaceous, 77 to 73 million years ago

Place: Alberta and Montana

Food: Plants

The Greatest Horns

Triceratops

Triceratops **was as big as a present-day African bull elephant.**

Too Fierce to Attack
The size, sharp horns, and armored neck frill of *Triceratops* would have put off most attackers.

First Fossils
The first fossils of *Triceratops* to be found were its horns. The scientist who studied them thought that they were the horns of some kind of Ice-Age bison.

FACTS AND FIGURES

Triceratops
(tri-SAIR-uh-tops)
Meaning of Name: "Three-horned face"
Classification: Ceratopsid
Size, Weight: 25 feet (8 meters) long, 6–7 tons (5,500–6,400 kilograms)
Time: Late Cretaceous, 68 to 65 million years ago
Place: Western United States and Canada
Food: Plants,

Triceratops had three **horns** on its head and a large armored neck frill. Many other kinds of dinosaur had lightly built skulls that fell to pieces before they could be preserved in the rock. An armored *Triceratops* skull, however, was so huge that it was often well-preserved.

In the 1990s, scientists found even bigger ceratopsid skulls—each 9 feet (about 3 meters) long—belonging to a *Pentaceratops* and a *Torosaurus*.

On the Move

Big horned dinosaurs, such as *Chasmosaurus* and *Pachyrhinosaurus*, were strong and muscular. They needed to be strong to carry the weight of their heavy neck frills and **horns** and to make long, seasonal journeys in search of new food supplies.

Chasmosaurus
Chasmosaurus **had a long skull. Most of this was made up of its neck frill. Holes in the frill helped to make it light. Muscular legs and powerful hips and shoulders helped the dinosaur carry its rhinoceros-sized body.**

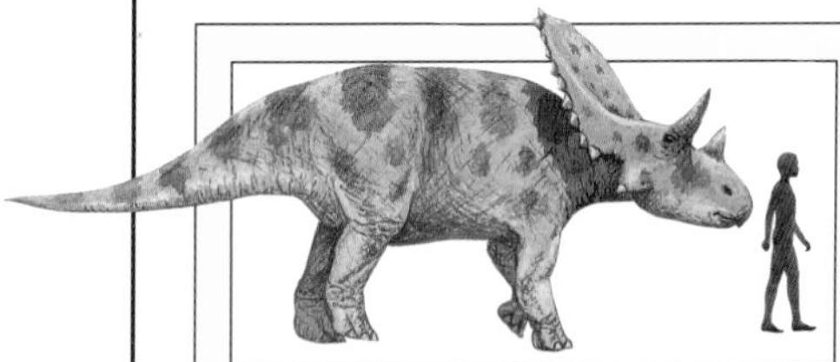

FACTS AND FIGURES

Chasmosaurus
(KAZ-mo-SAW-rus)
Meaning of Name: "Lizard with openings"–referring to the holes in the neck shield
Classification: Ceratopsid
Size, Weight: 17 feet (550 centimeters) long, 2–3 tons (1,800–2,700 kilograms)
Time: Late Cretaceous, 76 to 70 million years ago
Place: Alberta and Texas
Food: Plants

Digestive Organs
Chasmosaurus **had a large stomach and long intestines to help it digest tough plant food.**
Droppings of dung are sometimes preserved as fossils. They tell us what kind of food the dinosaur ate.

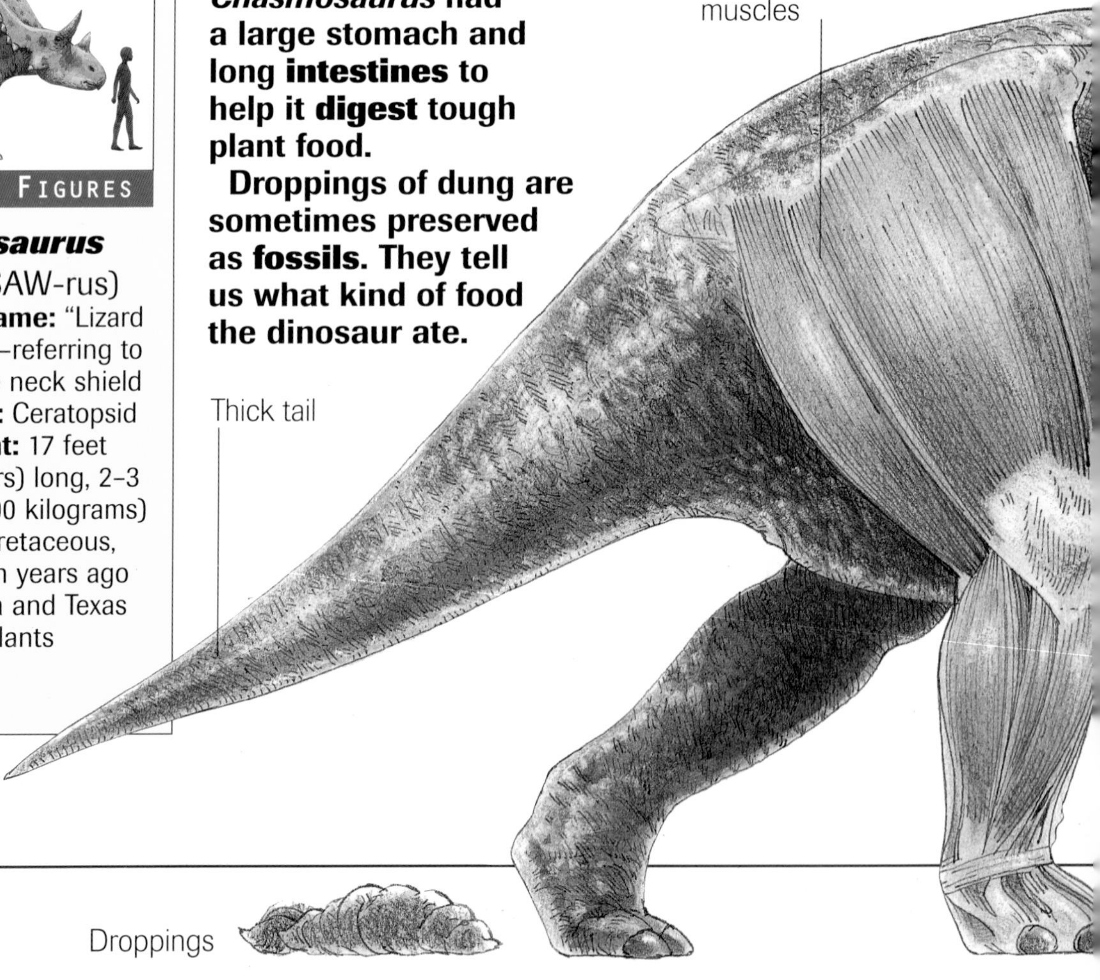

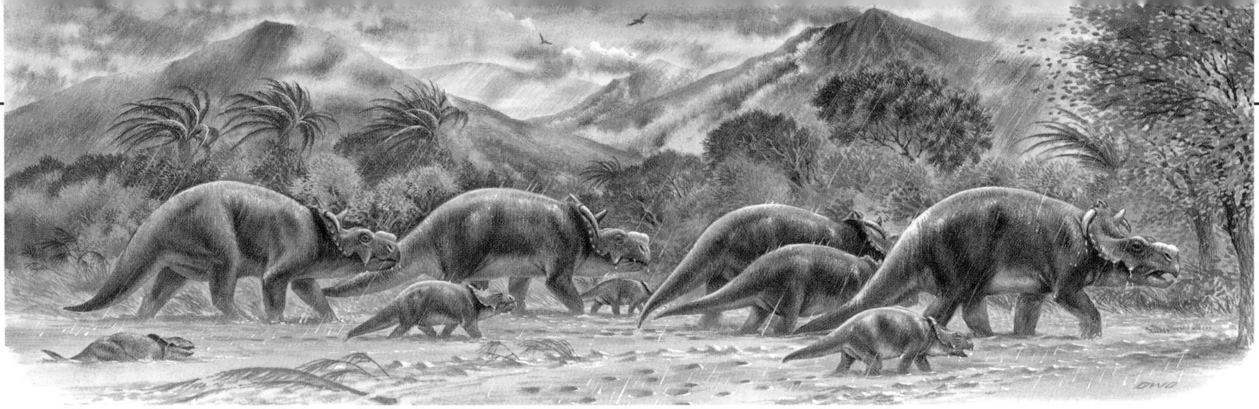

The bones of a herd of *Pachyrhinosaurus* were found in Alberta, Canada. The dinosaurs may have drowned in a flash flood as they crossed a river.

We know dinosaurs migrated because we have found vast "bone beds" of dinosaurs. These contain the **fossils** of many dinosaurs that all died together while they were on the move.

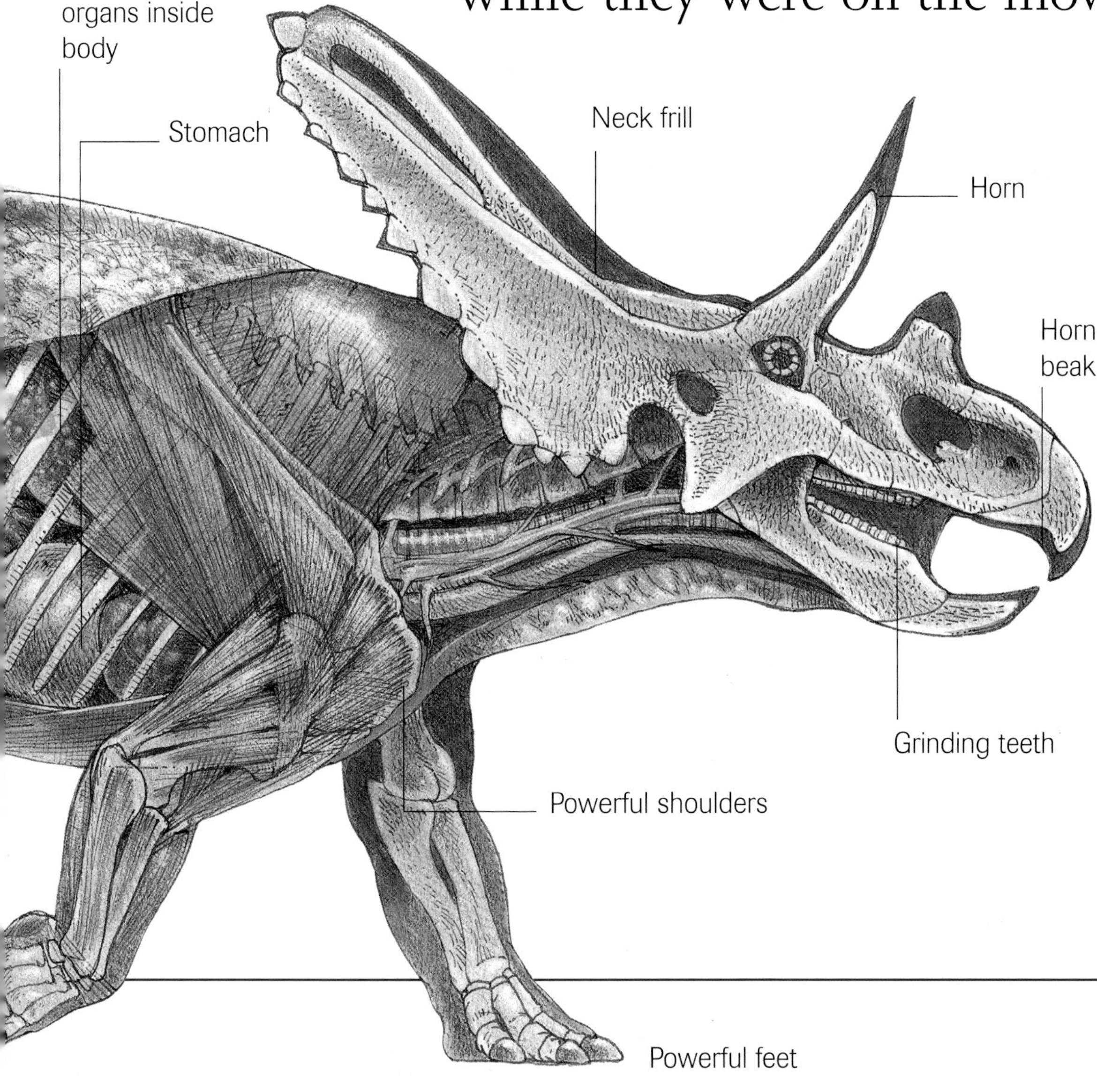

Two-Footed Plant-Eaters

For most of the Age of Dinosaurs, there were many types of plants. The most common type of plant-eating dinosaurs was a group called the **ornithopods**. The name ornithopod means "bird-footed" because the bones of the feet were arranged like those of a bird.

Herds of large and small plant-eating ornithopods wade into the shallow water at the mouth of a river to feed on horsetail plants. Nearby, a large meat-eater walks away with a fish it has caught, now clasped between its long, narrow jaws.

KEY
1 ***Baryonyx***
2 ***Iguanodon***
3 ***Hypsilophodon***

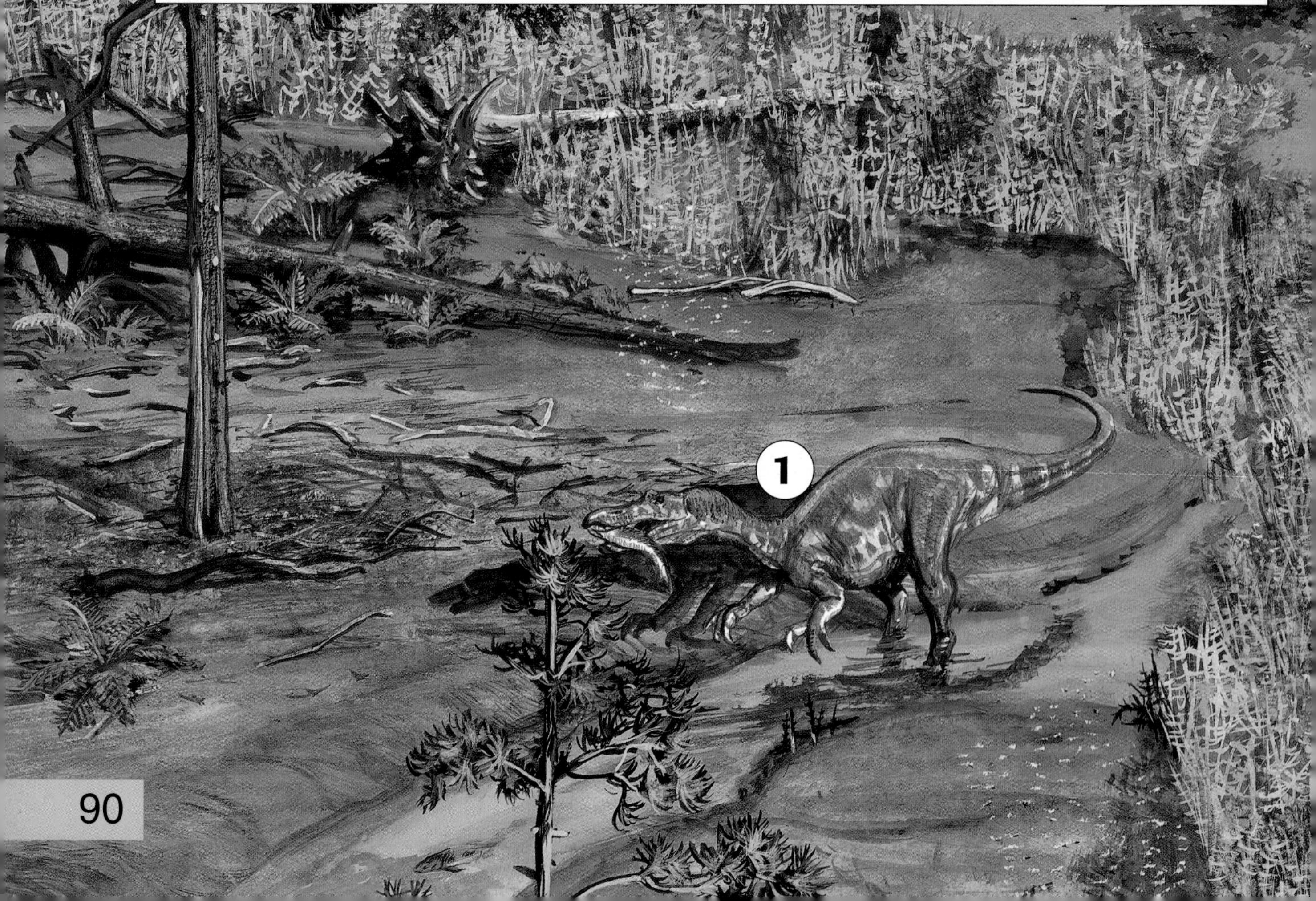

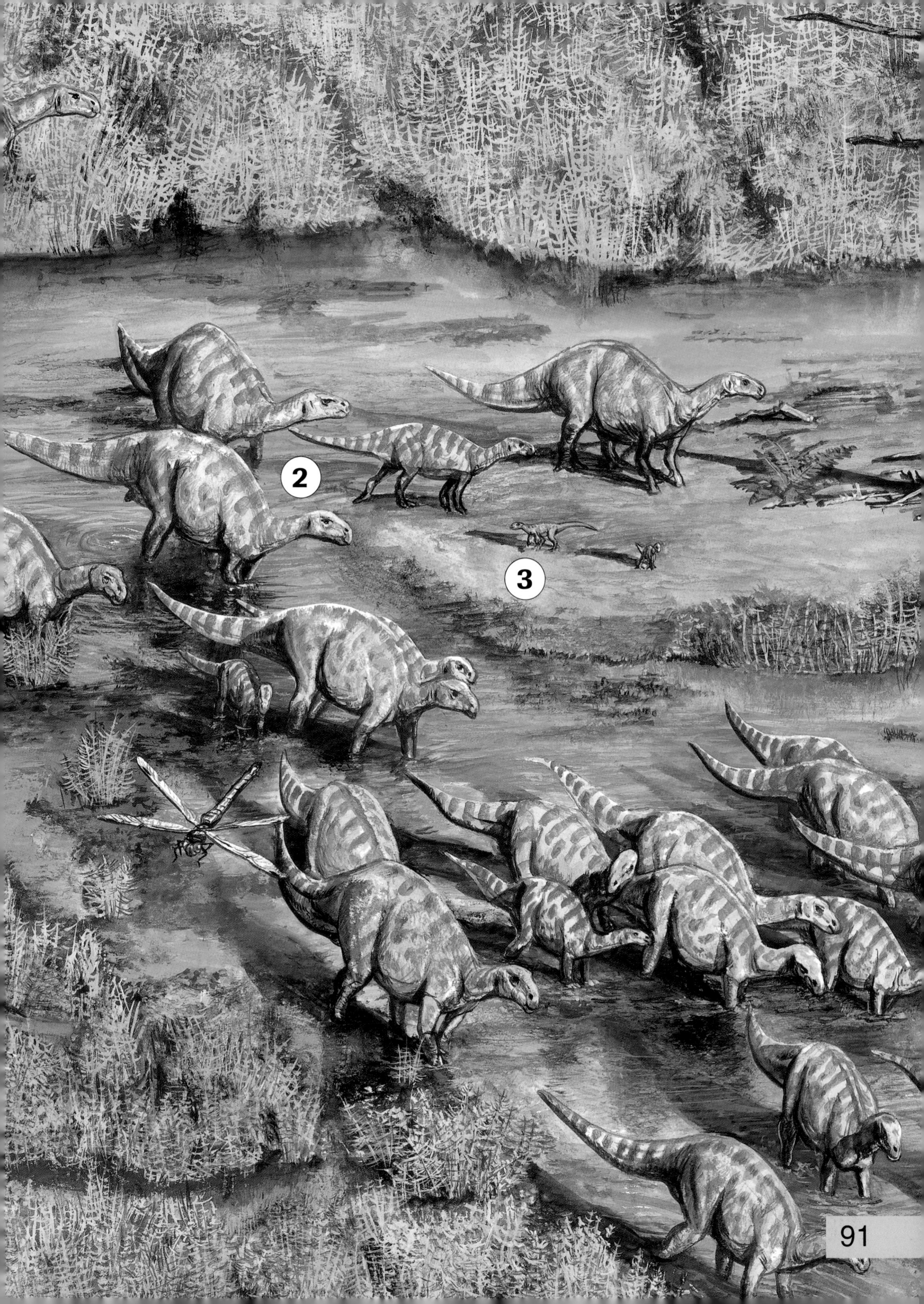

2
3

Early Examples

As in other dinosaur groups, the earliest **ornithopods** were quite small. They must have looked like large lizards running around on their hind legs rather than on all fours.

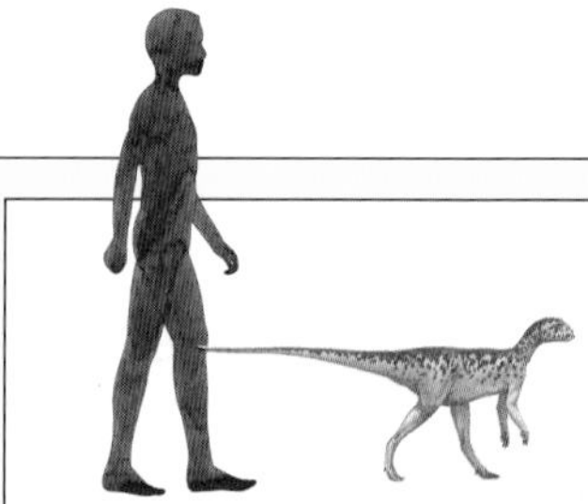

FACTS AND FIGURES

Heterodontosaurus
(HET-ur-oh-DON-toe-SAW-rus)
Meaning of Name: "Lizard with different kinds of teeth"
Classification: Heterodontosaur—one of the early ornithopod groups
Size, Weight: 3 feet (1 meter) long, 20 pounds (9 kilograms)
Time: Early Jurassic, 208 to 200 million years ago
Place: Southern Africa
Food: Plants, perhaps insects

Heterodontosaurus
***Heterodontosaurus* had a beak at the front of its mouth and cheek-pouches at the side, like all later ornithopods. It was different in that it had sharp fang-like teeth at the front and chewing teeth at the back.**

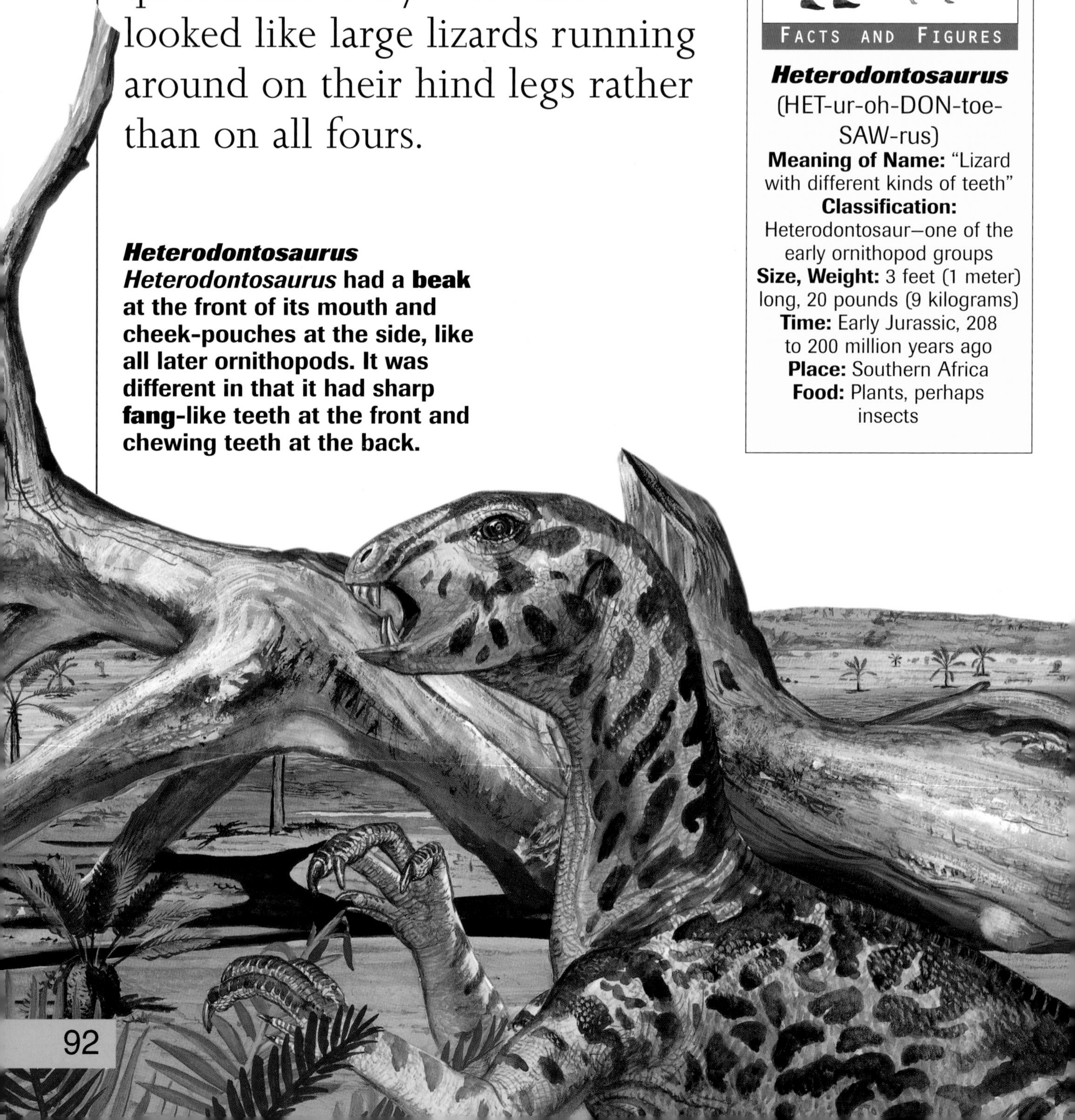

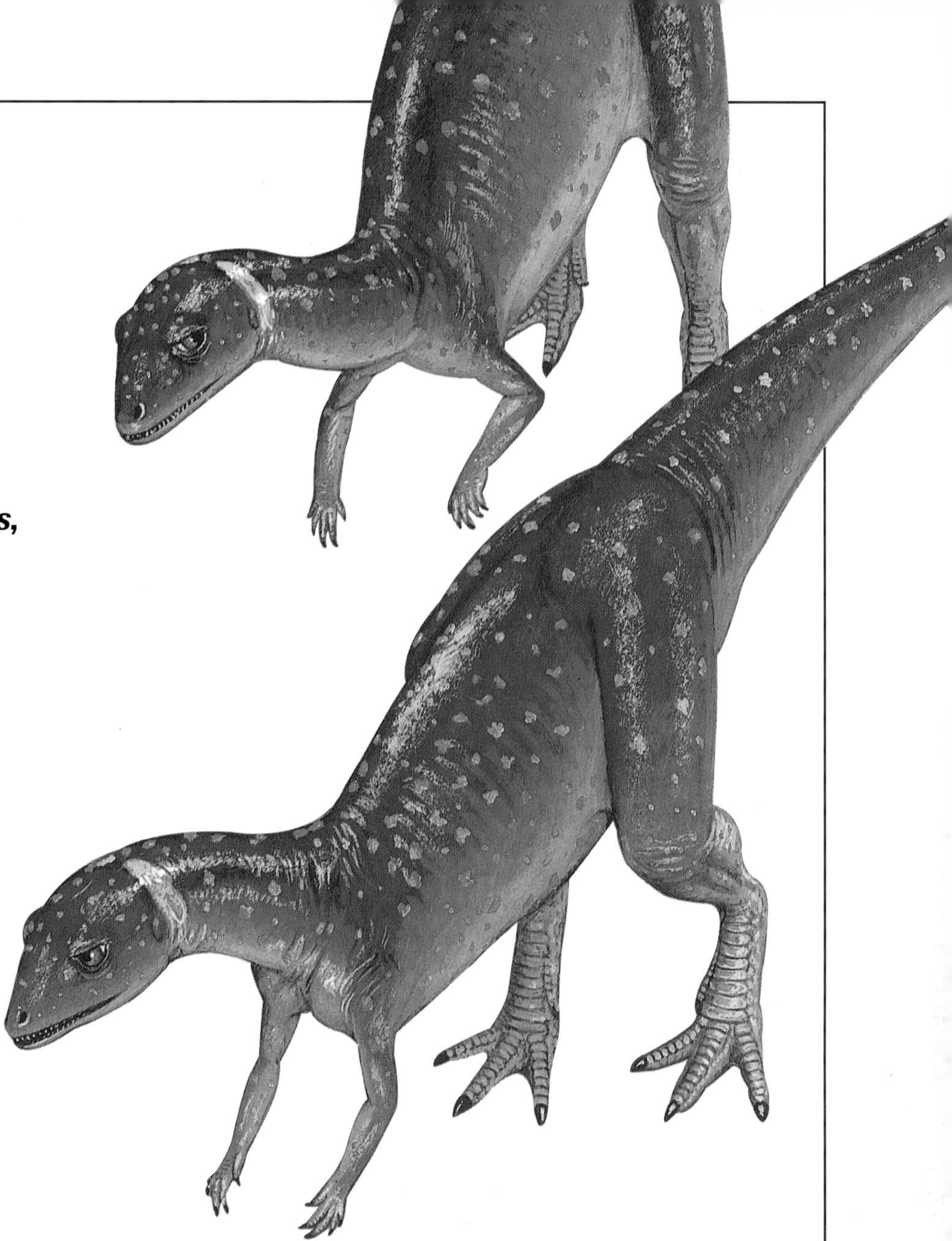

Lesothosaurus
Nearly all ornithopods had cheek-pouches that held their food while they chewed. But *Lesothosaurus*, an early ornithopod, had not developed these.

FACTS AND FIGURES

Lesothosaurus
(leh-SOO-too-SAW-rus)
Meaning of Name: "Lizard from Lesotho"—a country in southern Africa
Classification: Fabrosaur —a primitive group of ornithopods
Size, Weight: 3 feet (1 meter) long, 20 pounds (9 kilograms)
Time: Early Jurassic, 208 to 200 million years ago
Place: Southern Africa
Food: Plants, mostly ferns and horsetails

Two-footed plant-eating dinosaurs may have looked like meat-eaters, since they both walked on their hind legs. However, plant-eaters usually had larger bodies because they needed larger stomachs to **digest** their food.

Iguana-Tooth

The first remains of *Iguanodon* to be found were bone fragments and teeth. The teeth were very much like those of the modern iguana lizard, which is how *Iguanodon* got its name.

FACTS AND FIGURES

Iguanodon
(ih-GWAN-o-dahn)
Meaning of Name: "Iguana toothed"—teeth like those of an iguana lizard
Classification: Iguanodont
Size, Weight: 33 feet (10 meters) long, 7 tons ($6^1/_2$ tonnes)
Time: Early Cretaceous, 135 to 110 million years ago
Place: Western Europe and the western United States
Food: Plants

Iguanodon
Iguanodon **had large hind legs, three-toed feet, and shorter front legs with blunt hooves. It spent most of its time on all fours, but may have reared up on its hind legs to pull down branches.**

In the 1820s, when *Iguanodon* was discovered, people did not really know what dinosaurs were. Early drawings of *Iguanodon* made it look like a gigantic iguana. It was not until whole skeletons were found in 1878 that people could see its true shape.

Iguanodon Relatives
We know of many close relatives of _Iguanodon_. _Muttaburrasaurus_ lived in Australia, _Altirhinus_ lived in Asia, and _Ouranosaurus_ was found in Africa.

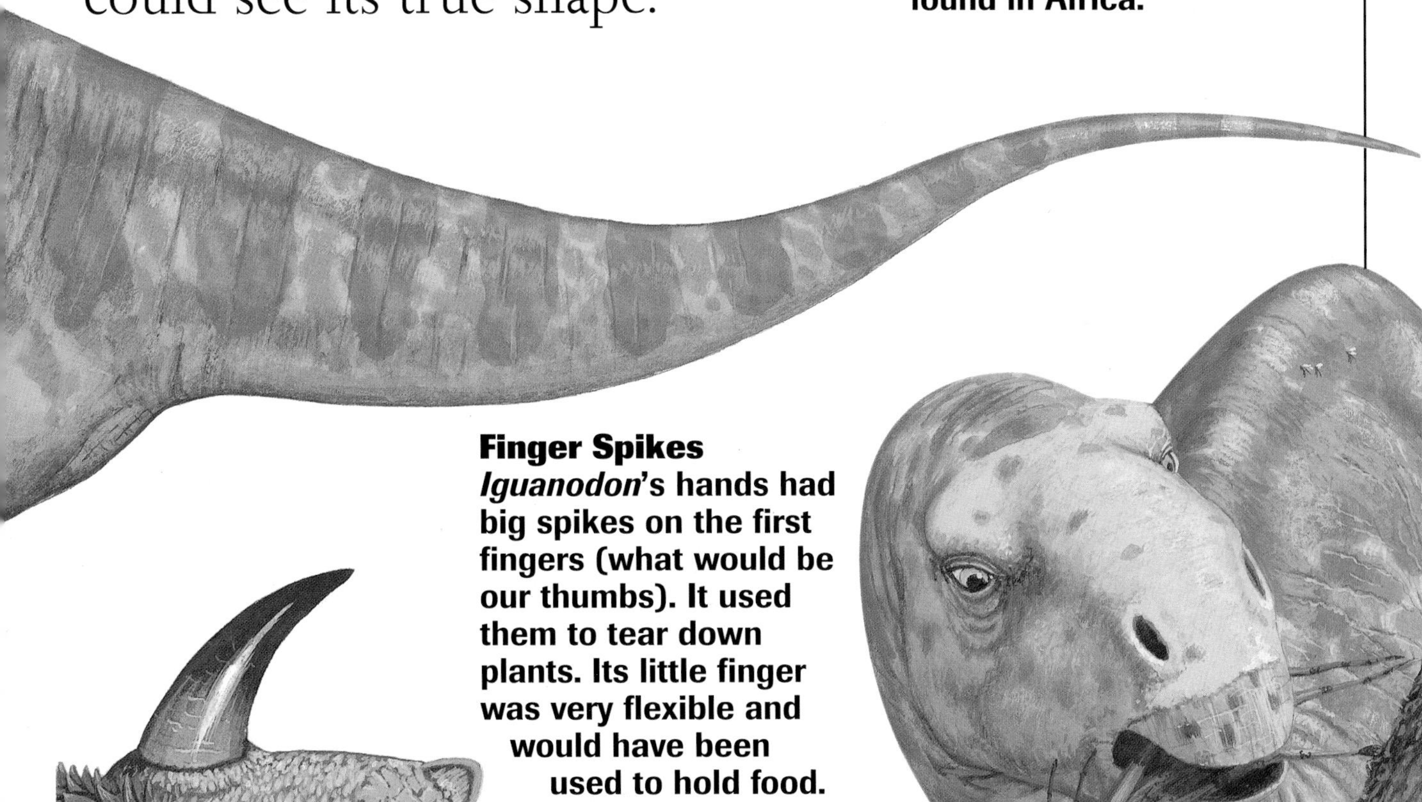

Finger Spikes
Iguanodon's hands had big spikes on the first fingers (what would be our thumbs). It used them to tear down plants. Its little finger was very flexible and would have been used to hold food.

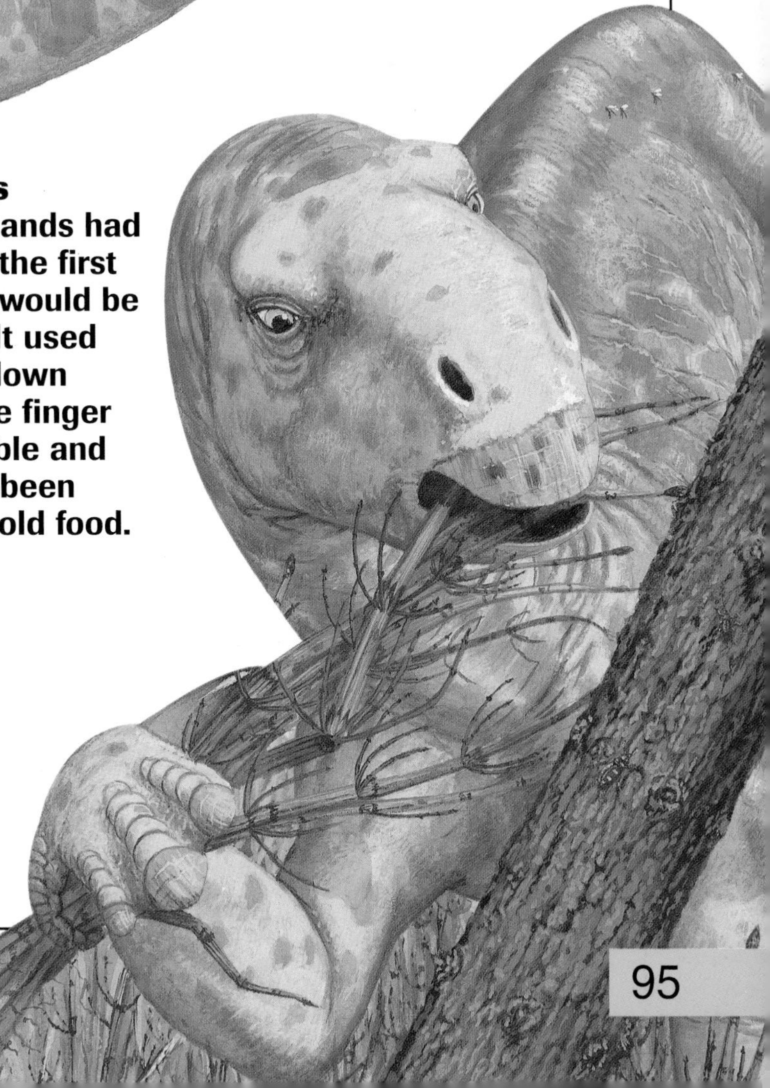

Boneheads

The boneheaded dinosaurs, or pachycephalosaurs, had a solid mass of bone on the top of their heads. They probably used these as battering rams, butting one another's heads to decide who would lead the herd, as mountain sheep do today.

Stygimoloch
As well as a dome of bone, *Stygimoloch* had spiky horns around the top of its head. The scientist who studied it and named it thought that *Stygimoloch* looked like a devil.

FACTS AND FIGURES

Stygimoloch
(STIG-i-MOL-uck)
Meaning of Name: "Demon of the river of death"
Classification: Pachycephalosaur—a group of two-legged plant-eaters with bony crowns
Size, Weight: 6 feet (2 meters) long, 50 pounds (23 kilograms)
Time: Late Cretaceous, 68 to 65 million years ago
Place: Montana
Food: Plants

Tylocephale
Scientists only know of part of the skull of *Tylocephale.* However, they can tell what the rest of the dinosaur's head looked like because the skulls of other pachycephalosaurs are well known.

FACTS AND FIGURES

Tylocephale
(TIE-lo-SEF-uh-lee)
Meaning of Name: "Lump-head"
Classification: Pachycephalosaur
Size, Weight: 8 feet (2½ meters) long, 100 pounds (45 kilograms)
Time: Late Cretaceous, 80 to 75 million years ago
Place: Mongolia
Food: Plants, perhaps low-growing mountain plants

Some scientists think that the boneheads' backbones were very strong, so when two boneheads crashed heads, the shock may not have badly damaged their bodies.

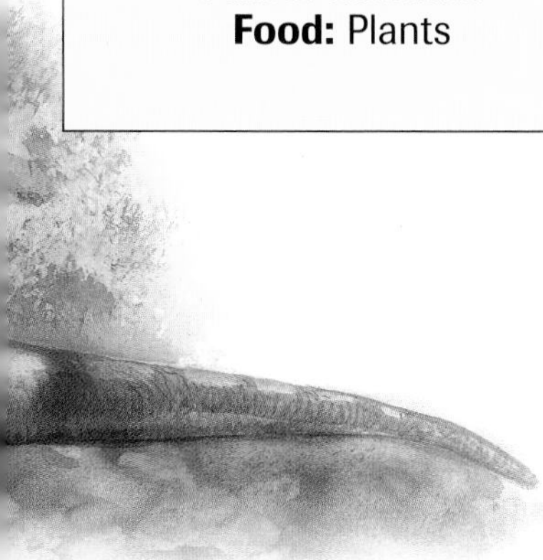

Fast Runners

The hypsilophodontids were the gazelles of the dinosaur world. They had slim bodies and long muscular legs. They would have been able to run away from danger very quickly.

Thescelosaurus
The hypsilophodonts existed until the very end of the Age of the Dinosaurs. *Thescelosaurus* was one of the last.

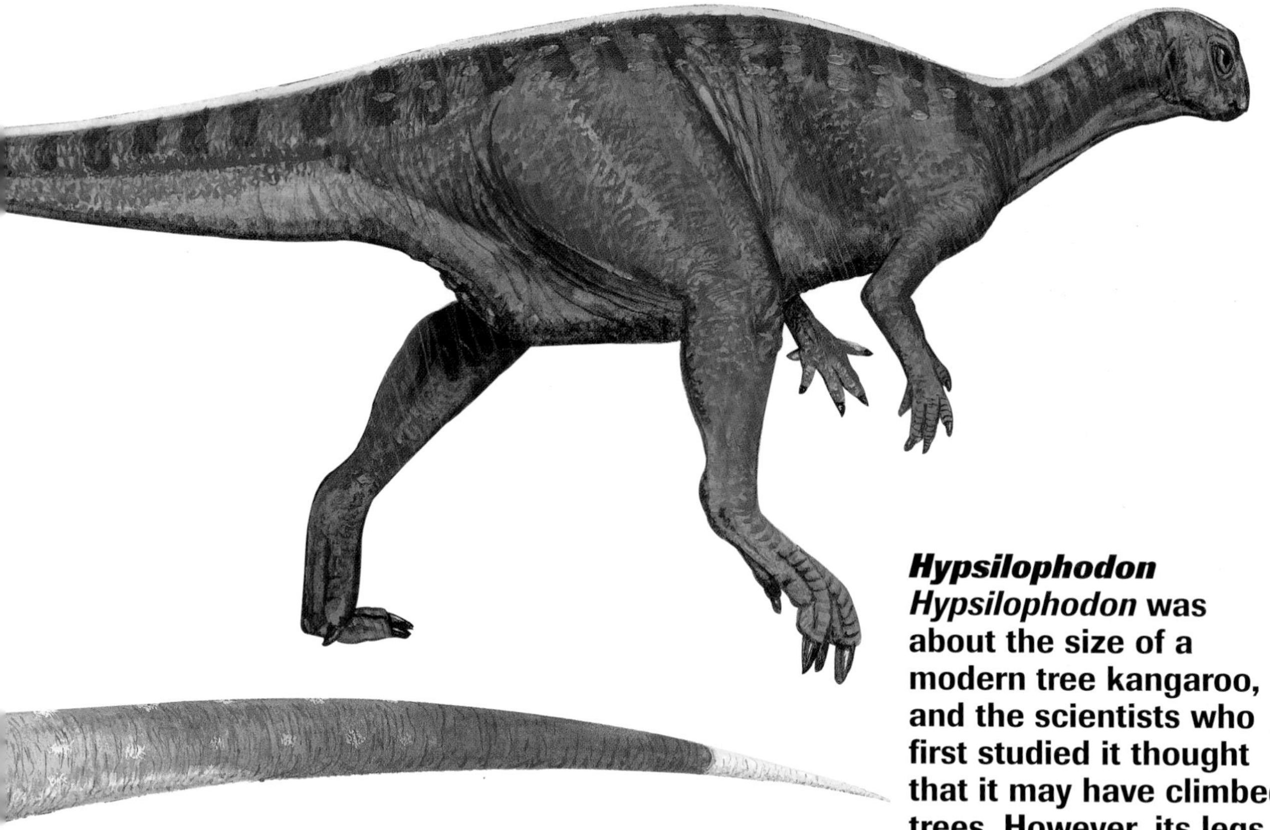

Hypsilophodon
Hypsilophodon **was about the size of a modern tree kangaroo, and the scientists who first studied it thought that it may have climbed trees. However, its legs were definitely those of a running animal.**

FACTS AND FIGURES

Thescelosaurus
(THES-ke-lo-SAW-rus)
Meaning of Name: "Marvelous lizard"
Classification: Hypsilophodont
Size, Weight: 11 feet ($3^1/_2$ meters) long, 100 pounds (45 kilograms)
Time: Late Cretaceous, 77 to 65 million years ago
Place: Western North America
Food: Plants, possibly selecting succulent shoots and buds

FACTS AND FIGURES

Hypsilophodon
(HIP-sih-LO-fo-dahn)
Meaning of Name: "High-ridged tooth"—from the shape of its teeth
Classification: Hypsilophodont
Size, Weight: 7 feet (2 meters) long, 60 pounds (27 kilograms)
Time: Early Cretaceous, 132 to 112 million years ago
Place: Southern England and Spain
Food: Plants

Living in the Cold

Ornithopod dinosaurs have now been found in Australia, in areas that would have been within the Antarctic Circle during the Early **Cretaceous** Period. This area was warmer than the Antarctic is today, but these dinosaurs must have been able to survive light frost, snow, and dark days during the Antarctic winter.

Leaellynasaura
The skull of this small dinosaur had big eye sockets. Large eyes must have helped it to see in the dark of the long winters.

Atlascopcosaurus
This dinosaur was named after the corporation that paid for the dig on which its remains were found.

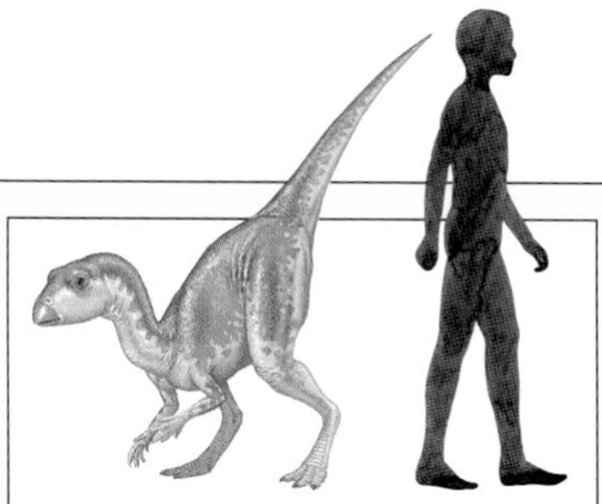

FACTS AND FIGURES

Leaellynasaura
(lay-EL-in-ah-SAW-rah)
Meaning of Name: "Leaellyn's lizard"—after Leaellyn Rich, the daughter of the discoverers, Tom and Patricia Rich
Classification: Hypsilophodont
Size, Weight: 6 feet (2 meters) long, 60 pounds (27 kilograms)
Time: Early Cretaceous, 115 to 110 million years ago
Place: Australia
Food: Plants

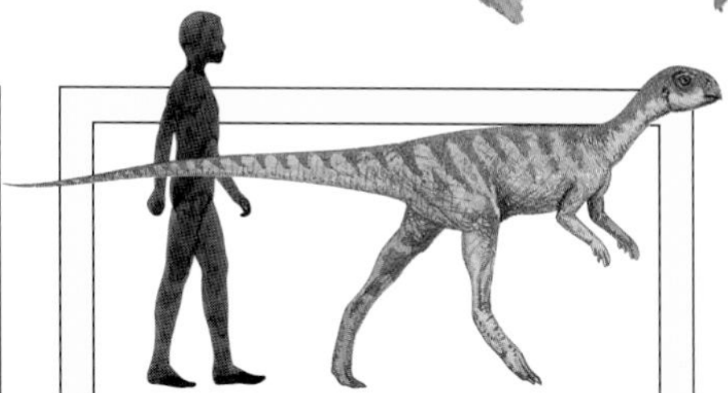

FACTS AND FIGURES

Atlascopcosaurus
(AT-lus-KOP-ko-SAW-rus)
Meaning of Name: "Lizard of the Atlas Copco Corporation"
Classification: Hypsilophodont
Size, Weight: 10 feet (3 meters) long, 100 pounds (45 kilograms)
Time: Early Cretaceous, 115 to 110 million years ago
Place: Southeast Australia
Food: Plants

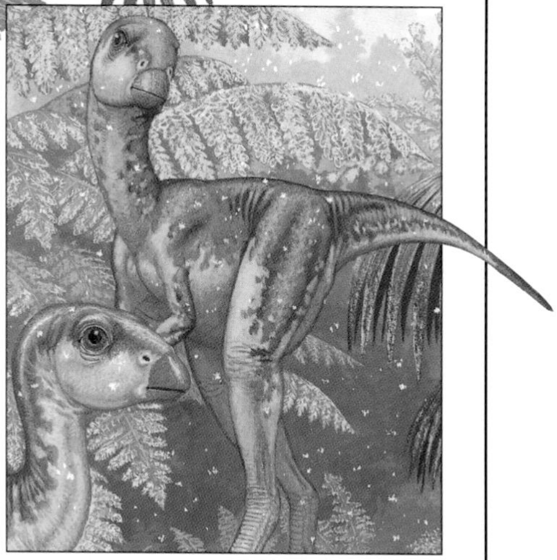

Cold-Climate Dinosaurs
We often think of dinosaurs living in hot jungles and deserts, so scientists were surprised to discover dinosaurs such as *Leaellynasaura* living in a cold climate.

Duckbills

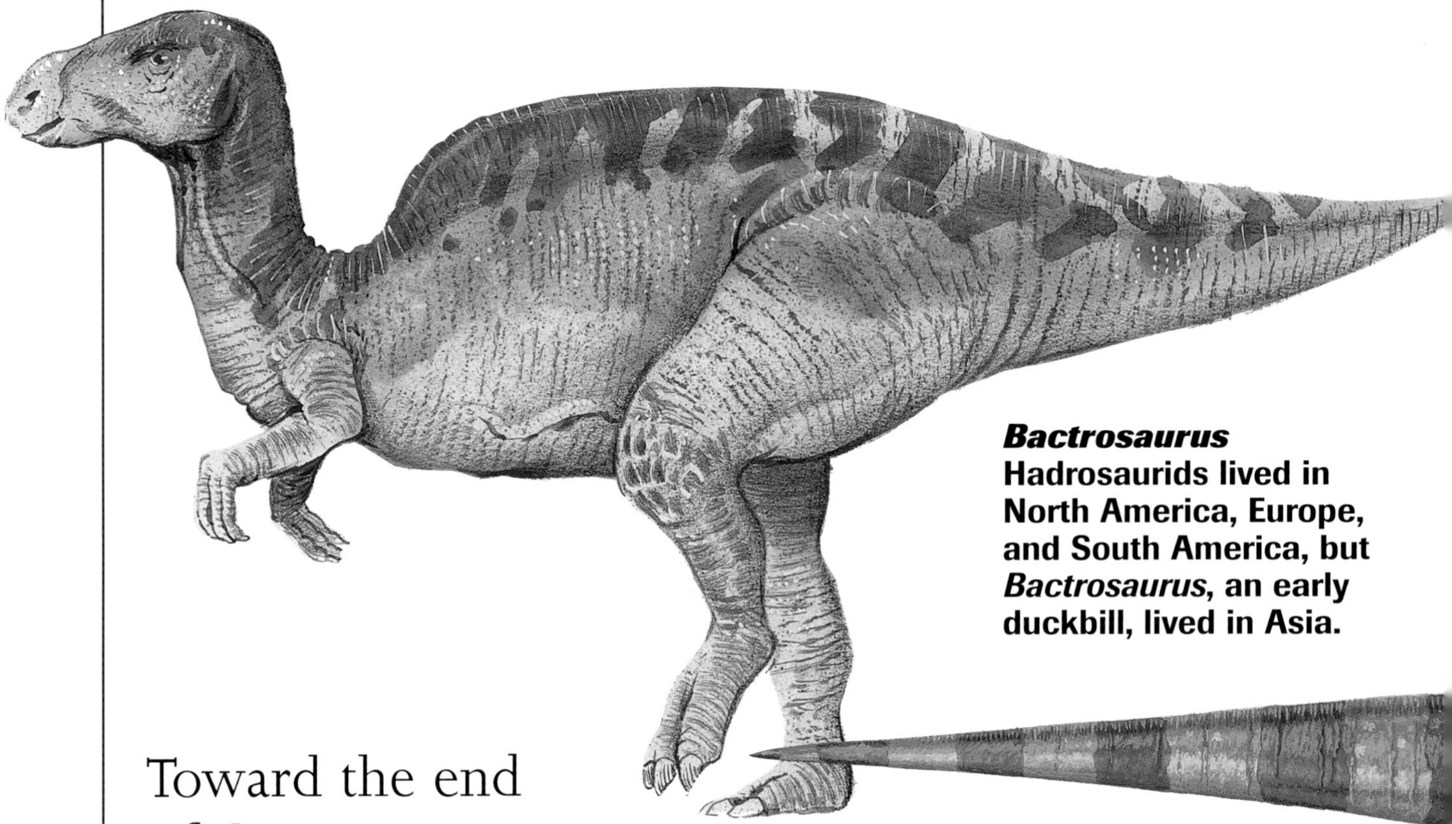

Bactrosaurus
Hadrosaurids lived in North America, Europe, and South America, but *Bactrosaurus*, an early duckbill, lived in Asia.

Toward the end of the **Cretaceous** Period, one group of **ornithopods** became the most important plant-eating dinosaurs. These were the hadrosaurs, or the duckbilled dinosaurs. They used their bills to scrape tough needles from **conifer trees.** Their jaws had hundreds of little teeth for grinding their food.

Earliest Duckbill
The earliest-known duckbill—*Eolambia*—was recently found in Utah. It lived during the Early Cretaceous Period. From *Eolambia*, the duckbills evolved and spread all over several continents.

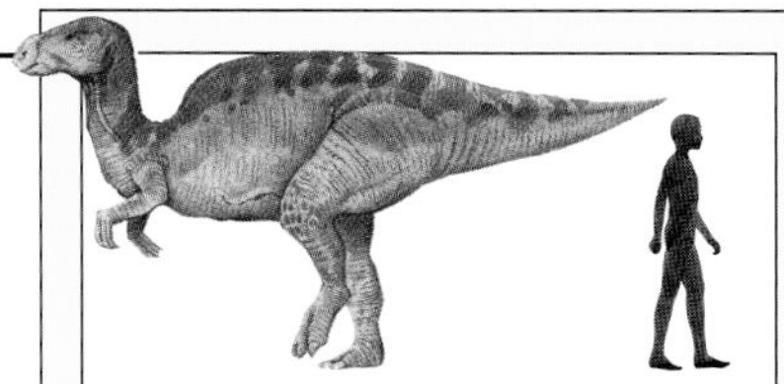

FACTS AND FIGURES

Bactrosaurus
(BACK-tro-SAW-rus)
Meaning of Name: "Lizard from Bactria"—a place in Asia
Classification: Hadrosaur—a group of ornithopods with ducklike beaks
Size, Weight: 20 feet (6 meters) long, 1 ton (900 kilograms)
Time: Late Cretaceous, 97 to 85 million years ago
Place: Mongolia and China
Food: Plants, especially conifers

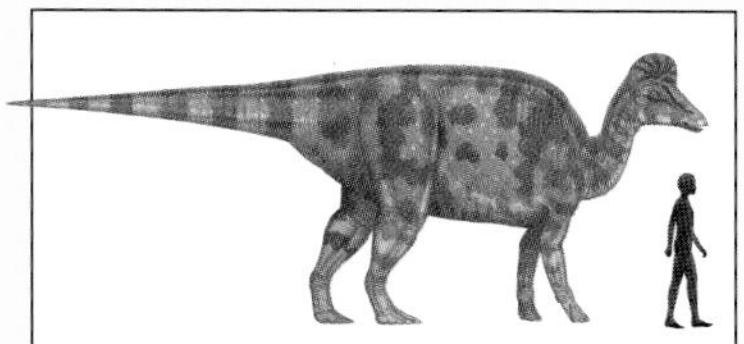

FACTS AND FIGURES

Hypacrosaurus
(hye-PACK-ro-SAW-rus)
Meaning of Name: "Almost the highest lizard"
Classification: Hadrosaur
Size, Weight: 33 feet (10 meters) long, 3 tons (2,700 kilograms)
Time: Late Cretaceous, 72 to 68 million years ago
Place: Alberta and Montana
Food: Plants, especially conifers

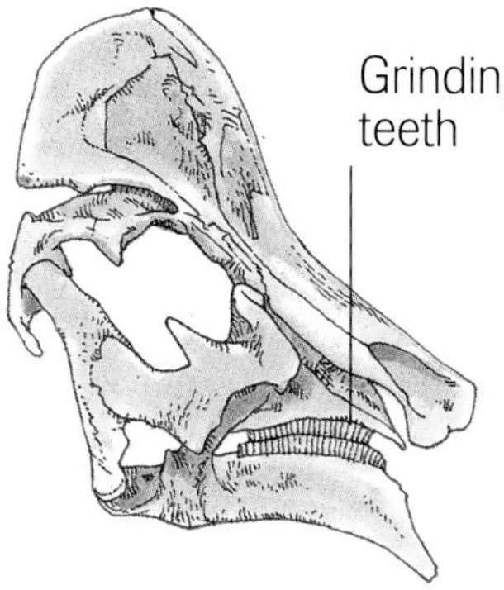

Hypacrosaurus
***Hypacrosaurus*'s skull contains forty rows of grinding teeth. These teeth were constantly being worn away and replaced by new ones. This shows that the duckbill ate tough vegetation.**

Showy Heads

Parasaurolophus
Parasaurolophus's **crest** consisted of curved and bent tubes. Air from the nostrils passing through this tube would have made a sound like that of a trombone.

Corythosaurus
Corythosaurus got its name from the shape of its rounded crest, which looks like the crest on the helmet of a Corinthian soldier of ancient Greece.

Lambeosaurus
The biggest and most spectacular crests may have been carried only by the males. Perhaps the crests were used mostly to attract a mate.

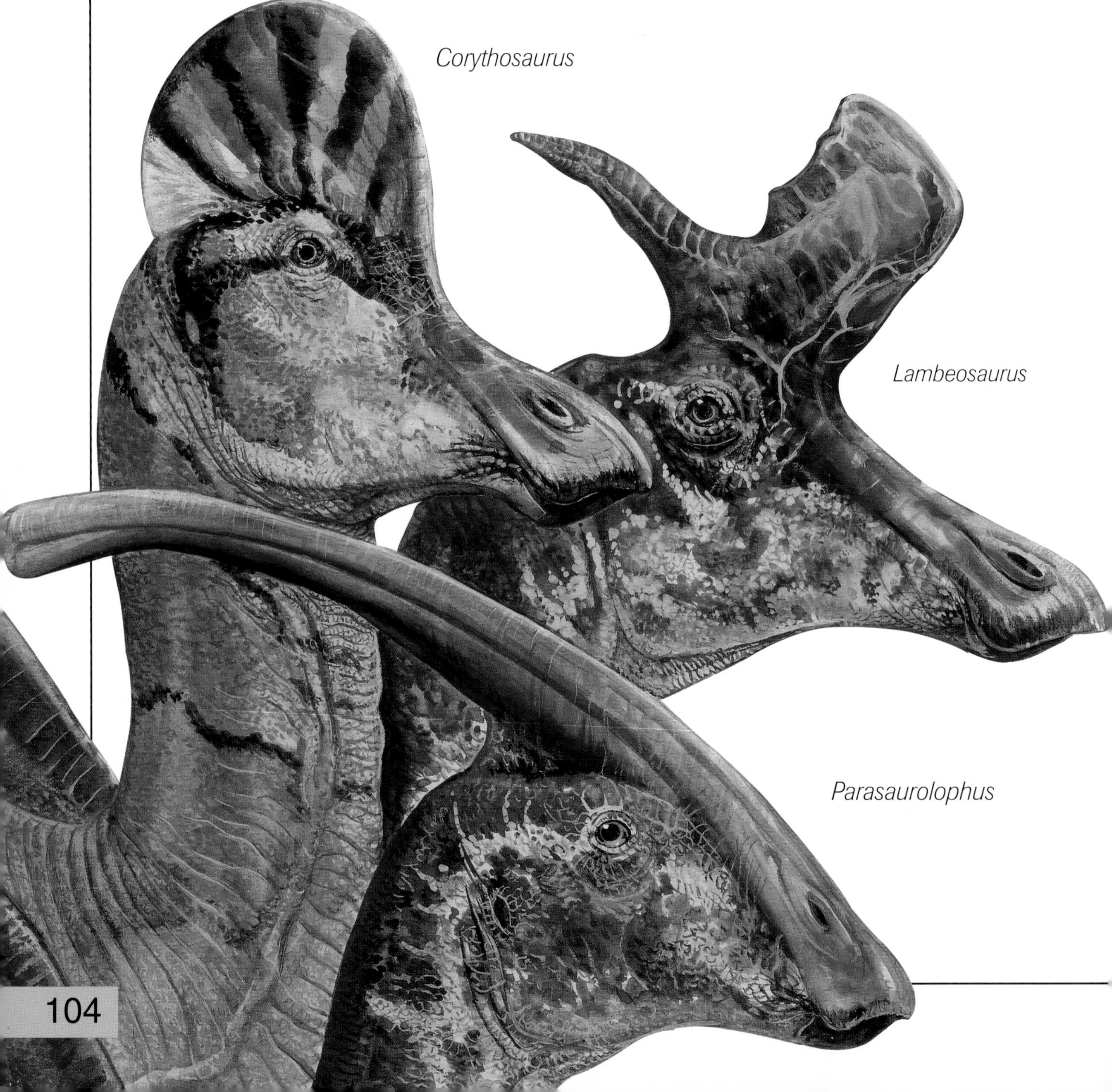

Some of the duckbills had large hollow **crests** on top of their heads. These were probably used to help the dinosaurs recognize one another. They may also have been used for signaling. We do not know whether dinosaurs could make noises, but we think crested dinosaurs communicated by honking or hooting. The sounds they made may have echoed through the forests.

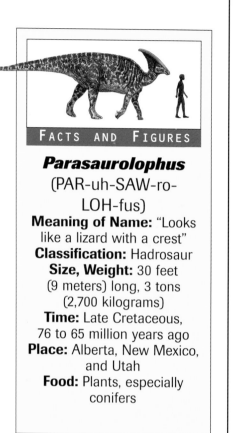

FACTS AND FIGURES

Parasaurolophus
(PAR-uh-SAW-ro-LOH-fus)
Meaning of Name: "Looks like a lizard with a crest"
Classification: Hadrosaur
Size, Weight: 30 feet (9 meters) long, 3 tons (2,700 kilograms)
Time: Late Cretaceous, 76 to 65 million years ago
Place: Alberta, New Mexico, and Utah
Food: Plants, especially conifers

FACTS AND FIGURES

Corythosaurus
(kor-ITH-o-SAW-rus)
Meaning of Name: "Lizard with a Corinthian helmet"
Classification: Hadrosaur
Size, Weight: 30 feet (9 meters) long, 3 tons (2,700 kilograms)
Time: Late Cretaceous, 76 to 72 million years ago
Place: Alberta
Food: Plants, especially conifers

FACTS AND FIGURES

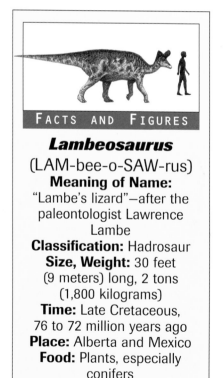

Lambeosaurus
(LAM-bee-o-SAW-rus)
Meaning of Name: "Lambe's lizard"—after the paleontologist Lawrence Lambe
Classification: Hadrosaur
Size, Weight: 30 feet (9 meters) long, 2 tons (1,800 kilograms)
Time: Late Cretaceous, 76 to 72 million years ago
Place: Alberta and Mexico
Food: Plants, especially conifers

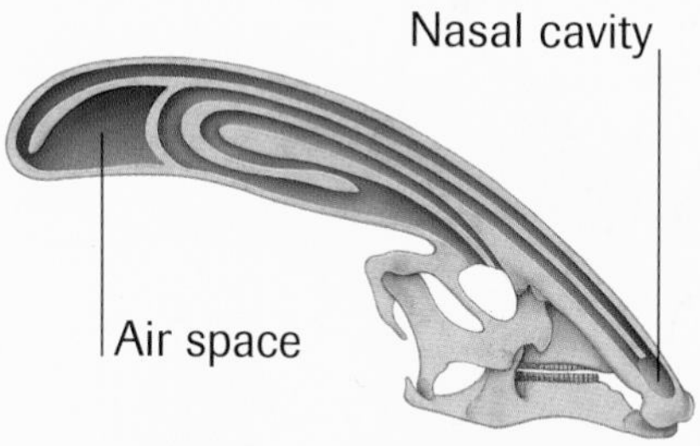

HONKS AND HOOTS

This *Parasaurolophus* skull shows the hollow channels running from the nose bones through the crest. Air from the nostrils had to pass through the channels before reaching the dinosaur's lungs. This would allow the dinosaur to honk or hoot loudly.

Nests and Eggs

Scientists know about the lifestyle of some dinosaurs because they have found **fossilized** nests containing eggs and youngsters. Some **ornithopods**, such as *Orodromeus*, lived in herds. Many females made nests together, in the same area, for protection.

Orodromeus Nests
Each *Orodromeus* nest was a mound of soil with a shallow hole scooped out of the top. Eggs were laid in the nest in a spiral pattern and may have been covered with **vegetation** to keep them warm. The **hatchlings** probably left the nest as soon as they hatched.

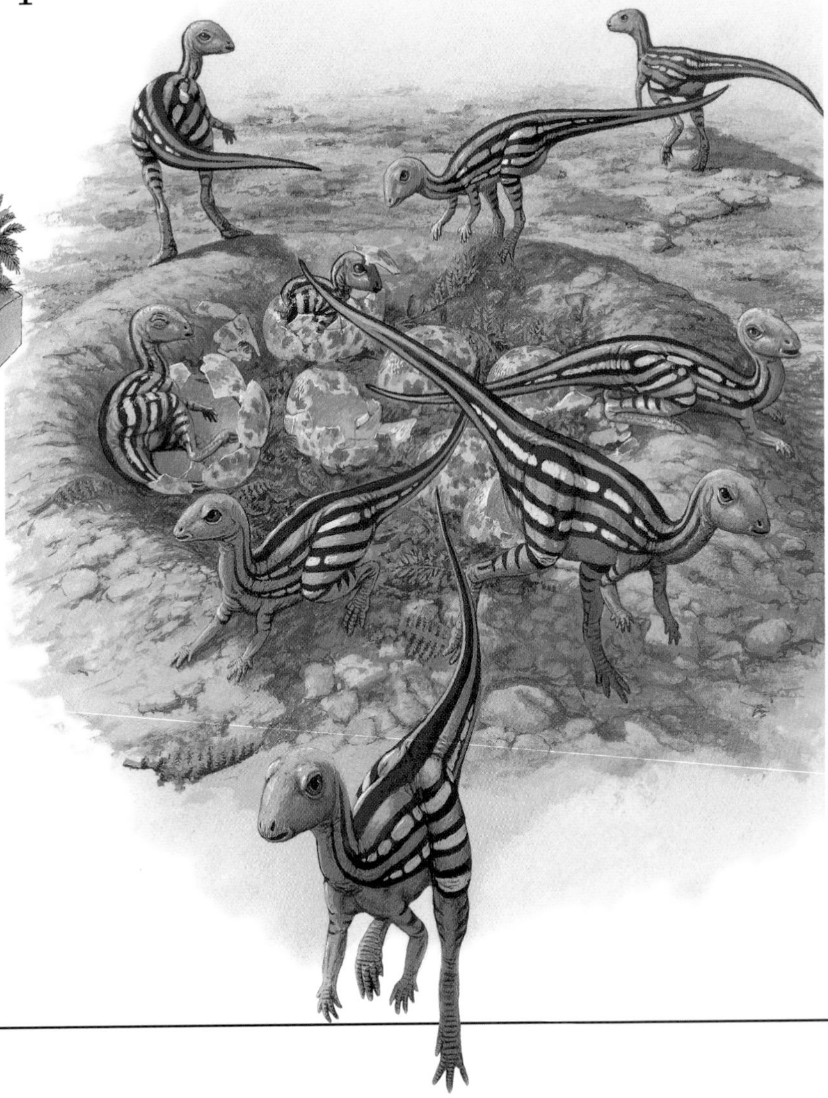

Nesting Colony
An *Orodromeus* nesting colony was found at Egg Mountain, in Montana. The nests were spaced apart so that there was room for each mother to walk around, and sit on, her nest without damaging the others.

Hatching Dinosaur
A dinosaur egg was like that of a modern reptile. The baby grew inside, feeding on the yolk. A protective membrane and a tough shell protected the growing baby. Some baby dinosaurs may have had a little horn on their noses, just as birds do. These would have helped them break out of the shell. The horns may have fallen off after a few days.

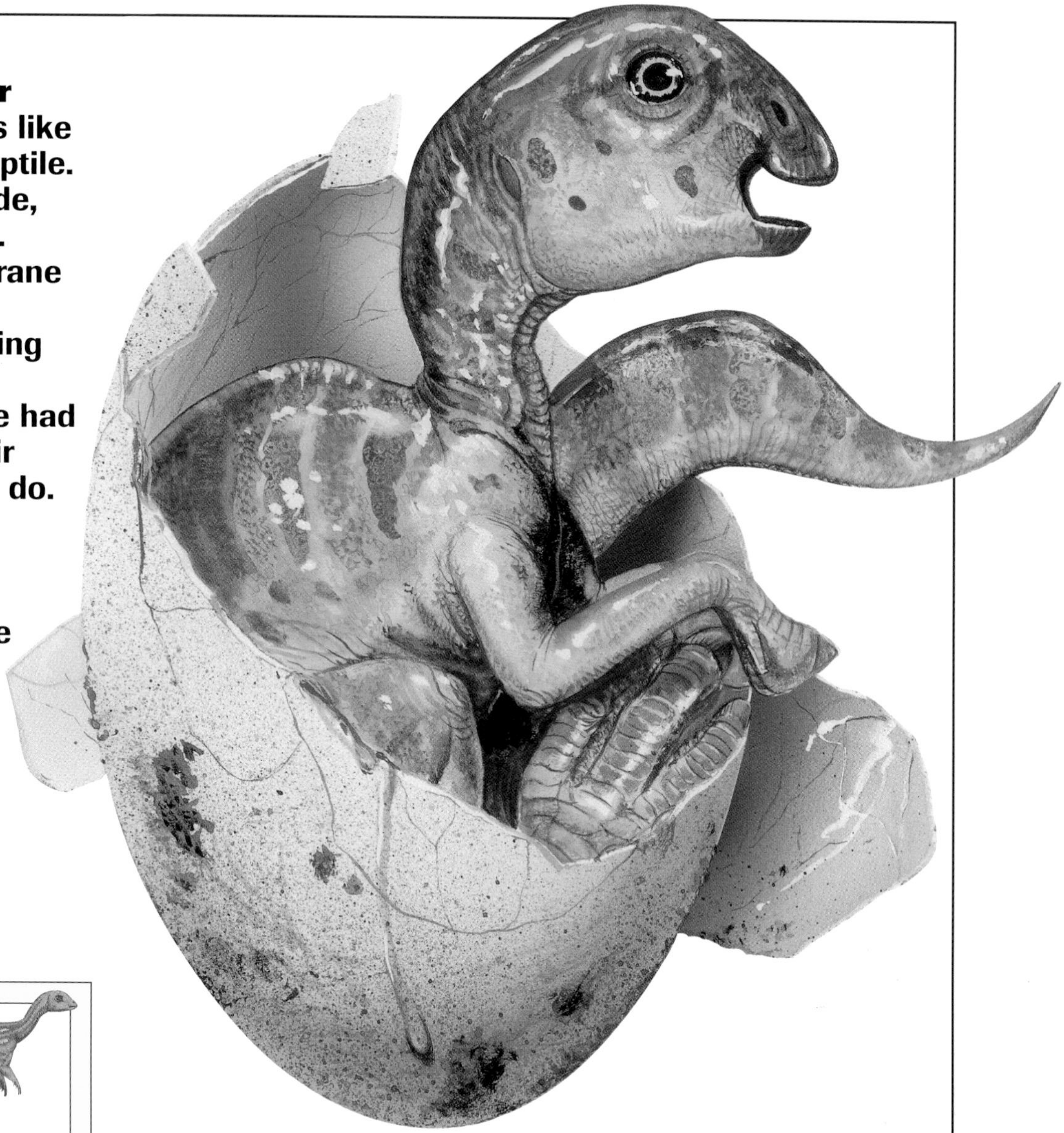

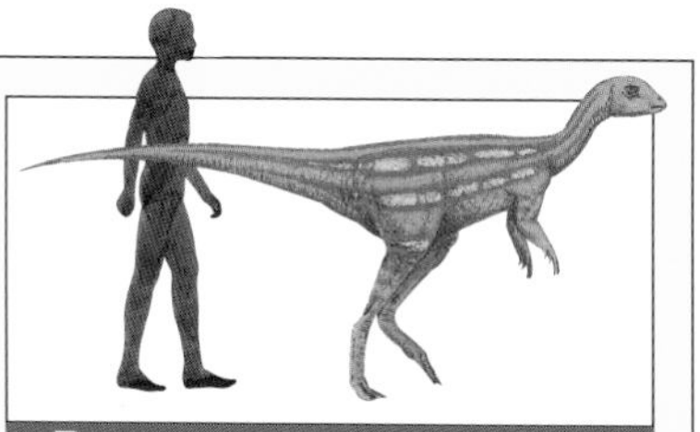

FACTS AND FIGURES

Orodromeus
(OR-o-DRO-mee-us)
Meaning of Name: "Mountain runner"
Classification: Hypsilophodont
Size, Weight: 8 feet ($2^1/_2$ meters) long, 66 pounds (30 kilograms)
Time: Late Cretaceous, 77 to 73 million years ago
Place: Montana
Food: Plants

Dinosaur eggs came in many sizes. The biggest were about the size of a soccer ball. Bigger eggs had to have thicker shells to hold their contents without cracking. If an egg were too big, a baby dinosaur would not be able to break out of the egg's thick shell.

Baby Dinosaurs

The duckbilled dinosaurs *Maiasaura* moved about in herds. They returned to the same nesting sites every year, as many birds do, and they brought up their youngsters there.

Keeping Safe
For the first few weeks of life, *Maiasaura* hatchlings would have stayed in or around the nest. Their parents would have brought them food and protected them from meat-eating animals.

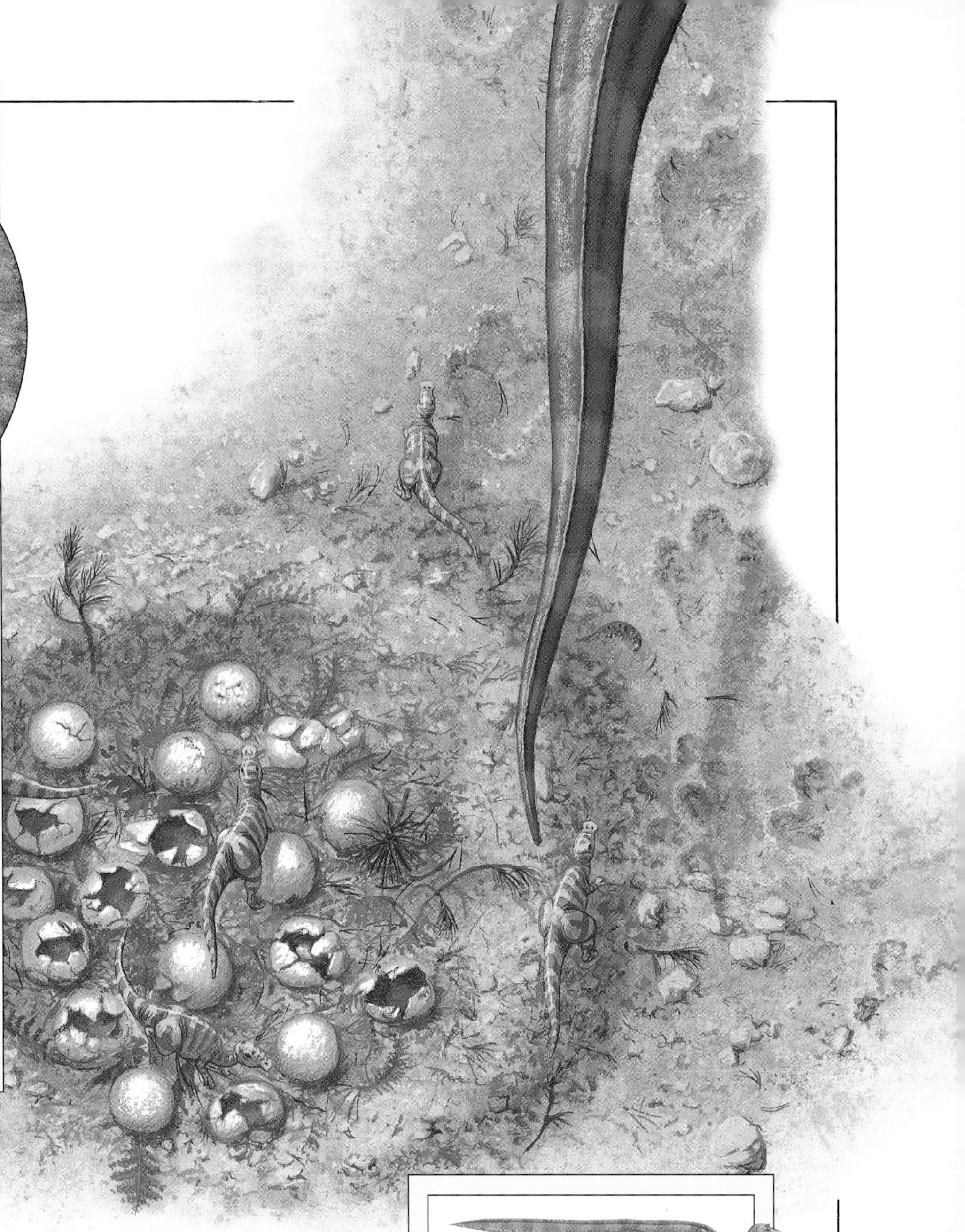

EGG LAYING

Dinosaur eggs were usually laid in a spiral pattern, with the narrow end pointing inward. The last egg laid was sometimes small and weak, as if the mother dinosaur had run out of energy by the time she had laid all her eggs.

The young *Maiasaura* probably stayed in the nest for a few months until they were partly grown. Their parents may have led them out of the nest from time to time so they could learn to find food for themselves.

FACTS AND FIGURES

Maiasaura
(MY-a-SAW-ra)
Meaning of Name: "Good mother lizard"
Classification: Hadrosaur
Size, Weight: 30 feet (9 meters) long, 3 tons (2,700 kilograms)
Time: Late Cretaceous, 77 to 73 million years ago
Place: Montana
Food: Plants

Safety in Speed

There were many fast-footed meat-eating dinosaurs during the Age of Dinosaurs. Many of the smaller **ornithopod** dinosaurs **evolved** into fast runners. They could escape from the larger meat-eaters.

Elaphrosaurus
***Elaphrosaurus* may have been an early type of dinosaur that looked like an ostrich. It was a slim-built, fast runner and must have been able to chase many of the other animals living at the time.**

KEY
1 *Elaphrosaurus*
2 *Dryosaurus*

It is easy to tell whether an animal was a runner from its skeleton. The legs have short thigh bones, where all the muscles were attached. The rest of the leg and the foot are long and slender. This makes the leg light in weight so it can be moved quickly while running.

Warm or Cold?

If a fast runner had been warm-blooded, it would have been able to run for a long time without getting tired. If it had been cold-blooded, it would have had to cool down and rest after a burst of speed.

Dryosaurus
***Dryosaurus*—like the hypsilophodonts—had legs that were built for speed. It had short thigh bones and long, light lower leg bones.**

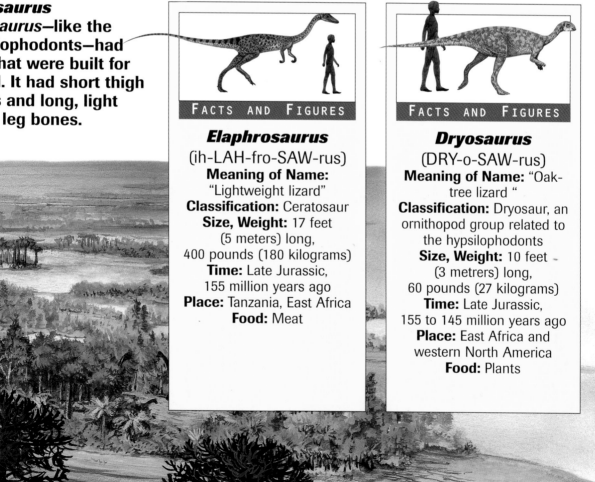

Facts and Figures

Elaphrosaurus
(ih-LAH-fro-SAW-rus)
Meaning of Name: "Lightweight lizard"
Classification: Ceratosaur
Size, Weight: 17 feet (5 meters) long, 400 pounds (180 kilograms)
Time: Late Jurassic, 155 million years ago
Place: Tanzania, East Africa
Food: Meat

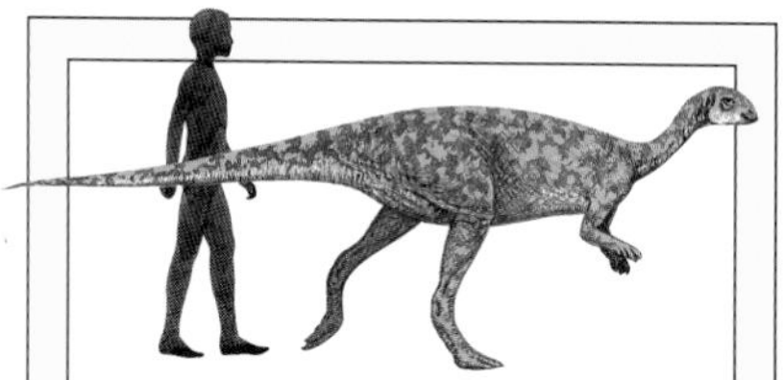

Facts and Figures

Dryosaurus
(DRY-o-SAW-rus)
Meaning of Name: "Oak-tree lizard "
Classification: Dryosaur, an ornithopod group related to the hypsilophodonts
Size, Weight: 10 feet (3 metres) long, 60 pounds (27 kilograms)
Time: Late Jurassic, 155 to 145 million years ago
Place: East Africa and western North America
Food: Plants

Safety in Numbers

The biggest meat-eating dinosaurs ate big plant-eaters. At the end of the **Cretaceous** Period, the duckbills were among the larger plant-eaters, and one of the biggest duckbills was *Edmontosaurus*. *Edmontosaurus* lived in herds. If a large meat-eater, such as a tyrannosaur, killed one of them, the rest of the herd would be safe for a few days while the meat-eater consumed its huge feast.

Meat-Eating Enemy
***Edmontosaurus* could easily be killed by *Tyrannosaurus*. The meat-eater's powerful teeth and strong jaws would have torn into the flesh of a cornered *Edmontosaurus*, giving it no escape.**

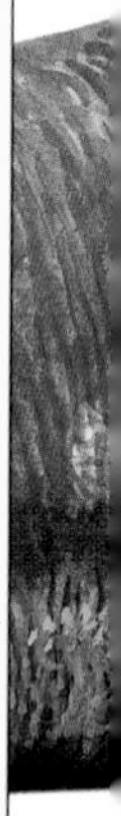

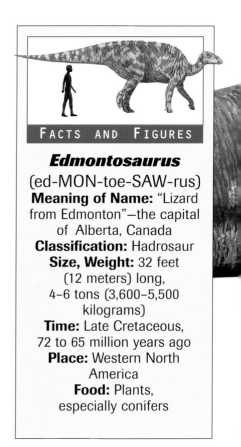

Facts and Figures

Edmontosaurus
(ed-MON-toe-SAW-rus)
Meaning of Name: "Lizard from Edmonton"—the capital of Alberta, Canada
Classification: Hadrosaur
Size, Weight: 32 feet (12 meters) long, 4–6 tons (3,600–5,500 kilograms)
Time: Late Cretaceous, 72 to 65 million years ago
Place: Western North America
Food: Plants, especially conifers

Scavenger or Predator?

Some scientists think that the biggest meat-eaters, such as *Tyrannosaurus*, chased and killed their own prey. Others think that they were scavengers, eating animals that had already been killed. Perhaps they were both. In either case, their prey would have been the plant-eating dinosaurs living at the time.

Edmontosaurus

Edmontosaurus **was one of the biggest, last, and best known of the hadrosaurs of North America. We know it from the many complete skeletons that have been found. We have even found preserved impressions of its skin, which are very rare for any dinosaur.**

Tyrannosaurus attacking an *Edmontosaurus*

Death and Decay

When an animal dies on land, its body is usually eaten by other animals, and the parts that cannot be eaten rot away. That is why we do not often find the whole preserved remains of dinosaurs.

Dinosaurs to Rocks
A herd of *Iguanodon* drown, and their bodies are washed down a river from the surrounding hills. The bodies of other dead animals are eaten by predators, but the *Iguanodon* bones, lying in a hollow, are not disturbed. The bones eventually turn to fossils and remain hidden for millions of years.

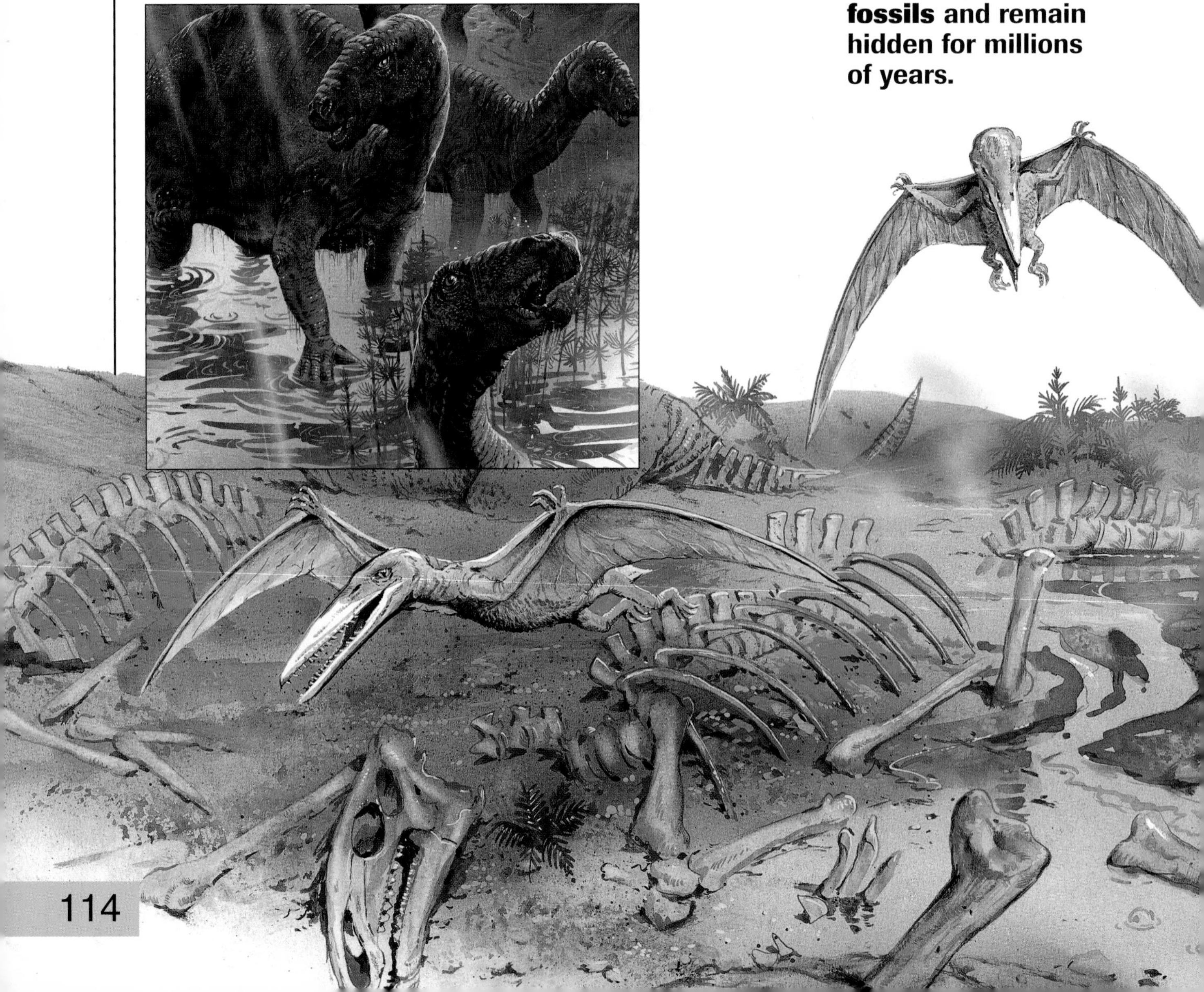

How a Fossil Skeleton was Formed

1 An *Iguanodon* dies by a muddy stream or drowns in a **flash flood.**

2 The meat and the other soft body parts rot away, leaving only the bones of the skeleton. The skeleton starts to get buried by mud and sand washed down by the stream.

3 After many years, the skeleton is buried under layers of **sediment.** Forces and pressure deep inside the Earth turn these layers into beds of rock, and the bones are filled with **minerals.**

4 The fossil skeleton lies hidden in rocks below our feet.

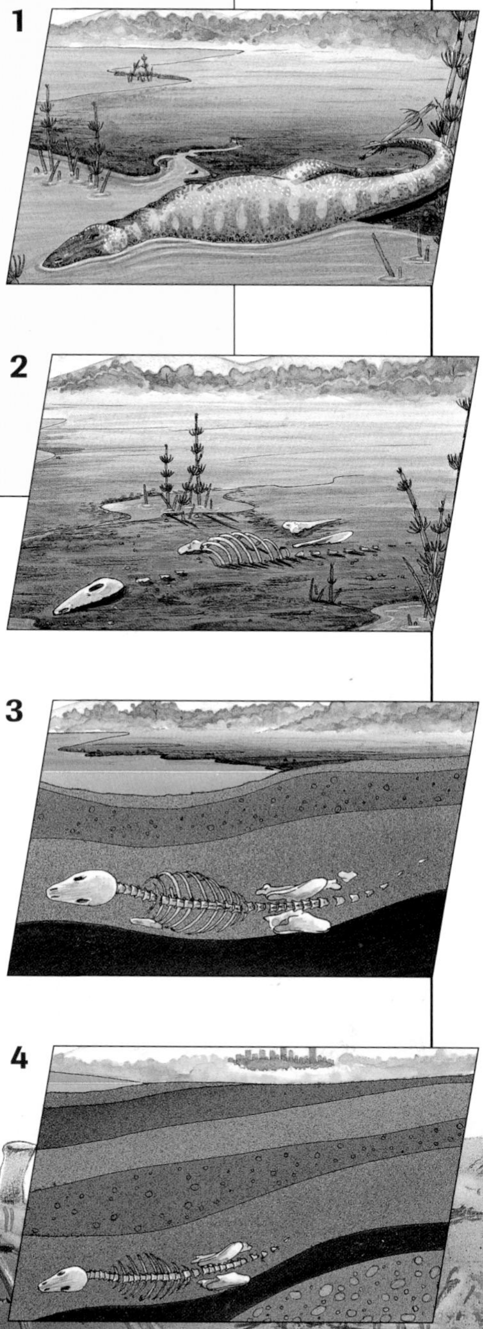

However, if a dinosaur fell into a river or lake and its body were quickly covered by mud and sand, other animals could not eat it. Then it would decay and become **fossilized**.

Discovery

Dinosaur **fossils** may remain buried in rock for millions of years. Sometimes, the rock above is worn away, and the fossils become exposed. Then they can be collected and studied by **paleontologists**, who try to find out about the life of the past.

Paleontologists
Paleontologists study maps to look for promising sites of dinosaur remains. Then, they may set out on scientific expeditions to try to find them.

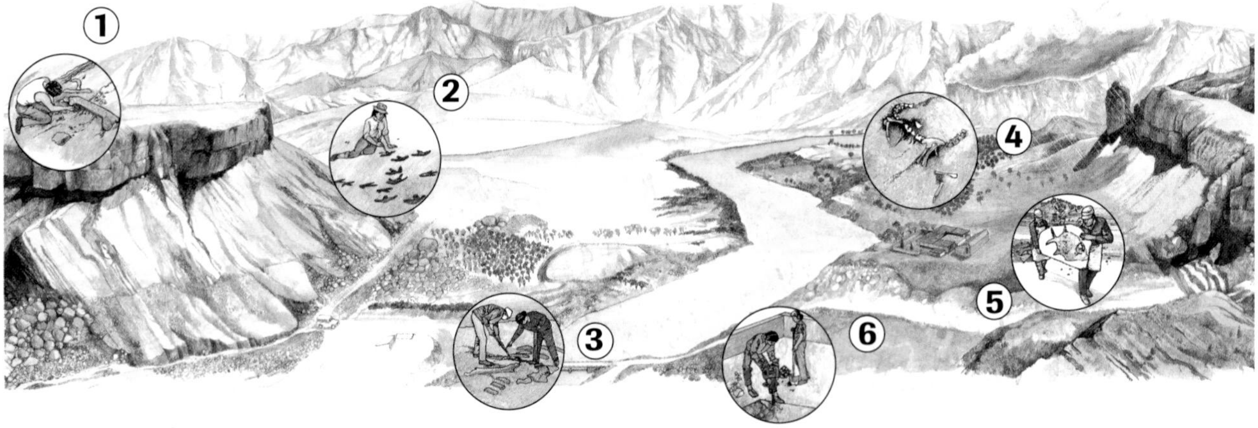

How Fossils Are Found

1 Some dinosaur skeletons are found by scientists. They know where to look because they have studied the types and ages of rocks in which they are likely to find dinosaur fossils.

2 Dry desert winds sometimes wear away rock, uncovering fossils.

3 Some fossils are washed out by rivers, which wear away the rocks.

4 If a fossil has been exposed naturally, by the wind or the rain, it is often found accidentally by people passing by.

5 and 6 When a new find is reported, paleontologists come and study the remains. They may cut the fossils out of the rock and take them back to a laboratory.

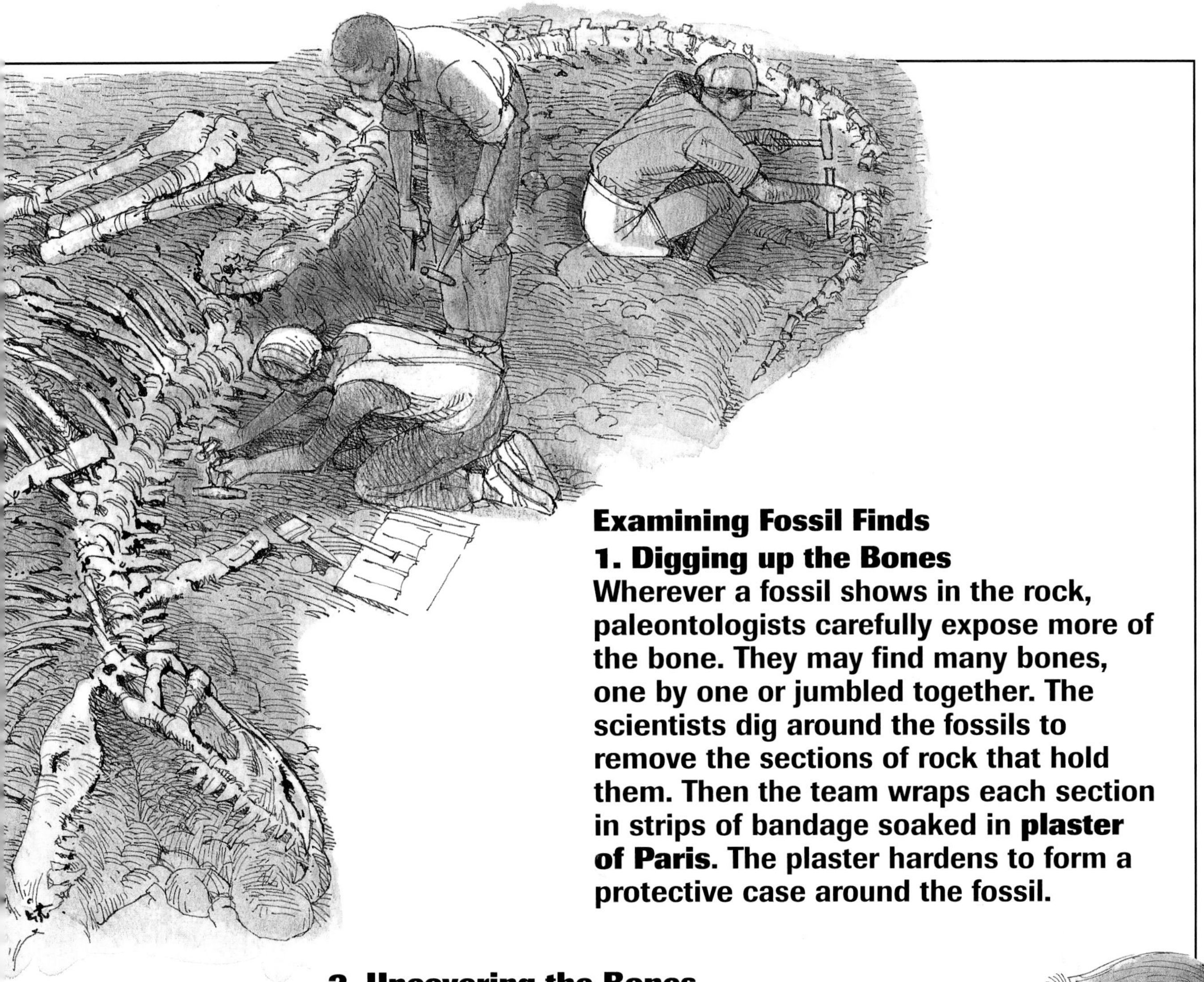

Examining Fossil Finds

1. Digging up the Bones

Wherever a fossil shows in the rock, paleontologists carefully expose more of the bone. They may find many bones, one by one or jumbled together. The scientists dig around the fossils to remove the sections of rock that hold them. Then the team wraps each section in strips of bandage soaked in **plaster of Paris**. The plaster hardens to form a protective case around the fossil.

2. Uncovering the Bones

At the museum, the protective cases are cut open. Then, skilled technicians called preparators use delicate tools to free each fossil from any remaining rock in which it is buried.

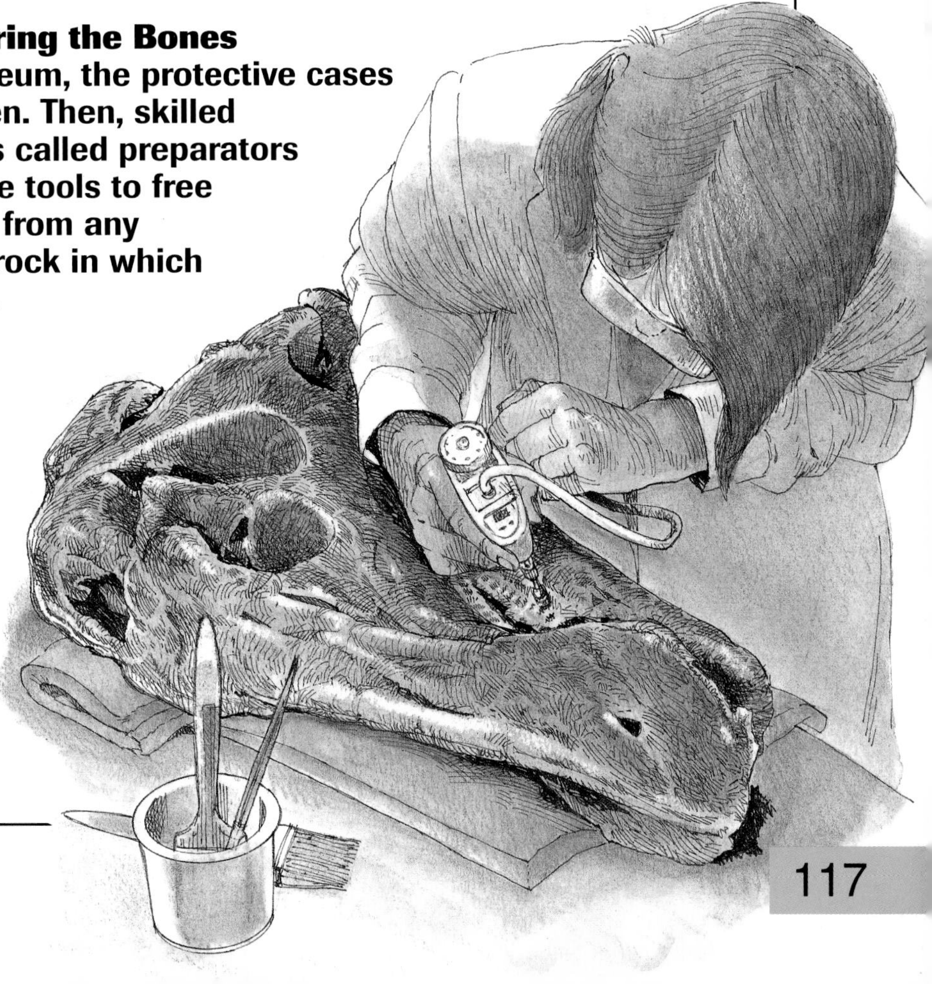

3. The Final Step

Separating the bones from the rock can take months, especially if the technicians have to use acid to eat away at the rock around the bones. Finally, the scientists can study the fossils and find out a little more about the dinosaurs.

Do You Know?

When did the dinosaurs first appear?
The earliest dinosaurs we now know are called *Eoraptor* and *Herrerasaurus*. These meat-eaters lived in South America at the start of the Late **Triassic** Period. They **evolved** from crocodile-like animals about 228 million years ago.

When did the dinosaurs die out?
Dinosaurs became extinct at the very end of the **Cretaceous** Period, about 65 million years ago. For a few million years before this, the numbers of dinosaurs had been getting smaller, but then suddenly all these animals, and many others, died out.

How are dinosaurs named?
A dinosaur's proper scientific name (in fact, the proper scientific name for all animals) consists of two parts. The first part, the genus, has a capital letter. The second part, the **species** name, does not. Both are written in italics or underlined. The first scientist to describe a new type of dinosaur usually gets to choose its name. The name is often taken from a person, a place, or a particular feature of the dinosaur.

How many kinds of dinosaurs are there?
Scientists know of more than 350 different genera of dinosaurs (genera is the plural of genus). This figure is probably just a quarter of all dinosaur genera that existed.

Which area had the most kinds of dinosaurs?
Most different kinds of dinosaurs are known from three main areas: the United States and Canada, Argentina in South America, and China and Mongolia.

Which were the most widely ranging dinosaurs?
Iguanodon, from the United States and various parts of Europe, was likely to have been one of the most widespread. Other wide-ranging dinosaurs included *Brachiosaurus* from Colorado and Tanzania; *Pachyrhinosaurus* from Alberta and Alaska; *Psittacosaurus* from China and Mongolia; and *Chasmosaurus* from Texas and Alberta.

Which was the tallest dinosaur?
Brachiosaurus, a long-necked **sauropod**, could have raised its head 40 feet (12 meters) above the ground.

Which was the heaviest dinosaur?
As far as we know, *Argentinosaurus* was the heaviest. In life, it would have weighed 100 tons (90 tonnes).

Which was the longest dinosaur?
Seismosaurus, meaning "earthquake lizard," was a sauropod, like *Diplodocus*. From the incomplete skeleton discovered in 1985, scientists think that the whole animal must have been 120–150 feet (37–45 meters) long.

Which was the most heavily armored dinosaur?
The **ankylosaurs**, such as *Euoplocephalus*, are regarded as the most heavily armored dinosaurs–they even had armored eyelids. The biggest, *Ankylosaurus*, was about 25 feet (8 meters) long. *Saichania* from Mongolia had armor on its belly as well as on its back.

Euoplocephalus

Which dinosaur had the biggest skull?
The **ceratopsians**, or horned dinosaurs with big frills covering their necks, had the biggest skulls. Some specimens of *Torosaurus* and *Pentaceratops* had a skull 9 feet (about 3 meters) long—that is the longest known of any land animal ever.

Which dinosaur had the biggest teeth?
Giganotosaurus had teeth that were more than 6 inches (15 centimeters) long. These are the biggest dinosaur teeth found.

Which dinosaur had the longest neck?
A complete skeleton of *Mamenchisaurus*, a *Diplodocus*-like sauropod from China, has a neck that is 36 feet (11 meters) long, the longest known of any animal. However, in 1987, scientists found the individual bones of a similar but larger animal. It would have had a neck nearly 50 feet (15 meters) long.

Which dinosaur had the biggest sail?
Spinosaurus was a meat-eater that may have been as big as *Tyrannosaurus*. On its back, it carried a **crest** that was supported by 5-foot-long ($1^1/_2$-meter-long) spines from its backbone.

Which dinosaur had the longest crest?
Parasaurolophus, one of the duckbilled dinosaurs, had a hollow crest that swept back from the skull a distance of 6 feet (about 2 meters).

Which dinosaur had the longest horns?
The three-horned dinosaur, *Triceratops*, had a **horn** on its nose and one over each eye. The bony cores of the eye horns were more than 3 feet (1 meter) long. They must have been much longer in life, when they would have had a covering of horn.

Which was the most intelligent dinosaur?
Troodon, a small meat-eater from Late Cretaceous Canada, may have been the most intelligent dinosaur. Its brain size, compared to the size of its body, was about the same as that of some modern birds.

Which was the fastest dinosaur?
A little, unknown dinosaur living in Arizona in the Early Jurassic Period left intriguing footprints in the rocks. The animal weighed about 20 pounds (9 kilograms), yet it made footprints that were about 12 feet ($3^1/_2$ meters) apart. The animal must have been running at 40 miles (64 kilometers) an hour.

Which was the smallest dinosaur?
At 3 feet (90 centimeters) long, a meat-eater called *Compsognathus* is the smallest adult dinosaur known. Young *Archaeoceratops* were only 2 feet (60 centimeters) long, but no one knows how big they were as adults.

Which were the longest-lived dinosaurs?
We cannot tell how long each dinosaur lived, but we think that the long-necked plant-eaters lived longer than the others. If they were **warm-blooded**, they may have lived to an age of 100 years. If they were **cold-blooded**, they may have survived for about 200 years.

Which museum has the most types of dinosaur?
The American Museum of Natural History in New York City has the most, with at least 100 different species.

Glossary

ankylosaur Armored dinosaur, such as *Euoplocephalus*, covered with bony spikes, knobs, and plates.

beak A horn-covered mouth structure with no teeth that occurs on birds and some dinosaurs. It is lighter than a set of teeth, and is used to gather food.

browse To feed on shoots, leaves, and bark of shrubs and trees.

camouflaged Having a natural color scheme or pattern that allows an animal to blend in with its surroundings so that it will not be noticed.

carnivores Meat-eating animals.

ceratopsian Horned dinosaur, such as *Triceratops*, with a sheet of bone, called a frill or shield, growing from the back of its skull.

cheek pouches Folds of skin and muscle at the sides of an animal's mouth that hold its food while it chews.

climate The average weather conditions in a particular part of the world.

cold-blooded Term used to describe an animal, such as a fish or a reptile, whose temperature changes from day to night and which needs less food than a warm-blooded animal.

conifer trees Trees that produce seeds in cones–for example, pines, firs, and larches. Their needle-like leaves usually stay on the trees all year.

continents The huge areas of land on Earth. The modern continents are (in order of size): Asia, Africa, North America, South America, Antarctica, Europe, and Australia.

crest A structure on top of the head, usually for display.

Cretaceous The final period of geological time between 146 and 65 million years ago. It was at the end of the Age of Dinosaurs.

cycad A plant related to the conifers consisting of a stout trunk and palm-like leaves.

digest To break down food in the stomach and intestines so that it can be absorbed by the body.

evolved Changed, over many generations, to produce new species.

fangs Long, pointed teeth.

ferns A plant that makes no flowers, with finely divided leaves known as fronds.

flash flood A sudden rush of water down a river valley following rainfall in nearby mountains.

fossilized Turned into fossils.

fossils Parts or traces of once-living plants or animals that are preserved in rocks.

ginkgoes Trees that look like conifers but with broad leaves that are shed in the fall. There is only one living species, the Maidenhair tree.

graze To eat low-growing plants. Sheep, cattle, deer, and other modern grazers eat grass. But there was no grass in dinosaur times.

hatchling An animal that is newly hatched from its egg.

herbivores Plant-eating animals.

hooves Very tough and heavy toenails built to take the weight of an animal.

horn Tough, shiny substance made of the same chemical material as hair, and often formed as a protective covering on some part of an animal. The name is also used for a pointed structure covered with horn.

horsetails Simple non-branching plants related to ferns, with segmented (or jointed) stems and tiny leaves.

impression Mark or print in the surface of the ground or a rock made by something pressing against or in it.

intestines The parts of the food canal below the stomach from which nutrients are absorbed into the blood for use by the cells and tissues of the body.

Jurassic The period of geological time between 208 and 146 million years ago. It was the middle period of the Age of Dinosaurs.

mammals Vertebrate (backboned) animals that produce live young and feed them on milk. Modern mammals include cats, dogs, mice, rabbits, whales, monkeys, and humans.

migrated Moved from place to place as conditions changed to find new sources of food or shelter or to mate and bring up young.

minerals Substances formed naturally in the ground. They include mixtures of elements such as iron, aluminum, potassium, carbon, silicon, oxygen, and hydrogen. All rocks are made up of minerals.

Ornitholestes grabs a young crocodile from its nest. *Ornitholestes* probably swallowed its prey whole.

ornithopod A two-footed plant-eating dinosaur, such as *Iguanodon*.

paleontologist A person who studies paleontology, the science of fossil life from early times.

plaster of Paris A mixture of fine powder (containing the mineral gypsum) and water that sets hard. It is used to protect a person's broken bones until they have healed.

predators Meat-eating animals that hunt and kill other animals for food.

prey An animal that is hunted and eaten by a predator.

pterosaur A flying reptile related to the dinosaurs. Pterosaurs flew using wings of skin stretched from the body to a single, long finger bone.

reptiles Cold-blooded vertebrate (backboned) animals that reproduce by laying hard-shelled or leathery eggs on land. Modern-day reptiles include snakes, lizards, turtles, and crocodiles.

sauropod A long-necked plant-eating dinosaur, such as *Brachiosaurus*, that walked on all fours.

scales In reptiles, small leaves of horn that form part of the outer covering of the body.

scavenger An animal that eats the bodies of animals that are already dead.

sediment Pieces of soil and rock carried by wind or water and deposited on the bottom of rivers, lakes, and streams.

species A group of living things in which individuals look like one another and breed with one another to produce young. Breeding, mating, and reproduction are all terms to describe the process by which individuals make more of their species.

stegosaur Armored dinosaur carrying a double row of pointed plates along its back. *Stegosaurus* is the best-known stegosaur.

tendons Tough pieces of animal tissue that attach muscles to bones.

theropod A meat-eating dinosaur, such as *Tyrannosaurus.*

tree ferns Plants of the fern family that grow to 80 feet (24 1/2 meters) or more in height. There are only a few living species, but they were plentiful at the beginning of the Age of Dinosaurs.

Triassic The period of geological time between 245 and 208 million years ago. The dinosaurs first appeared in the Triassic Period.

vegetation Plant life.

vestige A reduced structure or organ representing something that was once useful and developed.

warm-blooded Term used to describe an animal whose body temperature does not change from night to day and which needs large amounts of food.

Dilophosaurus attacks a small *Syntarsus*, another crested meat-eating dinosaur.

Index

E

F

G

H

Books to Read

An Alphabet of Dinosaurs by Peter Dodson. Scholastic Trade, 1995.

The Complete T. rex by John R. Horner and Don Lessem. Simon & Schuster, 1993.

Digging Dinosaurs: The Search That Unraveled the Mystery of Baby Dinosaurs by James Gorman, John R. Horner, and David Attenborough. Harper Perennial Library, 1996.

Diggin' Up Tyrannosaurus rex by J. R. Horner and D. Lessem. Crown, 1994.

The Dinosaur Data Book: The Definitive Illustrated Encyclopedia of Dinosaurs and Other Prehistoric Reptiles by David Lambert. Random House, 1998.

The Dinosaurs of North America: An Odyssey in Time by Dale Russell. NorthWord Press, Inc., 1989.

Dinosaur Worlds: New Dinosaurs, New Discoveries by Don Lessem. Boyds Mills Press, 1996.

Dougal Dixon's Dinosaurs by Dougal Dixon. Boyds Mills Press, (Updated) 1998.

Hunting Dinosaurs by Louis Psihoyos. Random House, New York, 1994.

The Newest and Coolest Dinosaurs by Philip J. Currie, Colleayn O. Mastin, Jan Sovak. Grasshopper Books, 1998.

The Ultimate Dinosaur Book by David Lambert. Dorling Kindersley, 1993.

Troodon, The Smartest Dinosaur; *Seismosaurus, The Longest Dinosaur*; and *Utahraptor, the Nastiest Dinosaur*–all by Don Lessem. Carolrhoda Books, 1996.

Where to Find Dinosaurs Today by Daniel and Susan Cohen. Puffin, 1992.

Tyrannosaurus, one of the last of the dinosaurs.